Exploring Education Through Phenomenology

Exploring Education Through Phenomenology

Diverse Approaches

Edited by
Gloria Dall'Alba

WILEY-BLACKWELL

A John Wiley & Sons, Ltd., Publication

This edition first published 2009
Originally published as Volume 41, Issue 1 of *Educational Philosophy and Theory*, except for
chapter 4 ("Schools as Places of Unselving: An Educational Pathology?") newly written by
Michael Bonnett
Chapters © 2009 The Authors
Book compilation © 2009 Philosophy of Education Society of Australasia

Blackwell Publishing was acquired by John Wiley & Sons in February 2007. Blackwell's
publishing program has been merged with Wiley's global Scientific, Technical, and Medical
business to form Wiley-Blackwell.

Registered Office
John Wiley & Sons Ltd, The Atrium, Southern Gate, Chichester, West Sussex, PO19 8SQ,
United Kingdom

Editorial Offices
350 Main Street, Malden, MA 02148-5020, USA
9600 Garsington Road, Oxford, OX4 2DQ, UK
The Atrium, Southern Gate, Chichester, West Sussex, PO19 8SQ, UK

For details of our global editorial offices, for customer services, and for information about
how to apply for permission to reuse the copyright material in this book please see our
website at www.wiley.com/wiley-blackwell.

Library of Congress Cataloging-in-Publication Data

Exploring education through phenomenology : diverse approaches / edited by
Gloria Dall'Alba.
      p. cm.
   Includes bibliographical references and index.
   ISBN 978-1-4051-9659-8 (pbk. : alk. paper) 1. Education–Philosophy. 2. Phenomenology.
I. Dall'Alba, Gloria.
   LB14.7.E965 2009
   370.1–dc22

                                    2009021975

A catalogue record for this book is available from the British Library.

Set in 10pt Plantin by Graphicraft Limited, Hong Kong
Printed and bound in Malaysia by Vivar Printing Sdn Bhd

01   2009

Contents

Notes on Contributors

Catherine Adams is an assistant professor of education, career and technology studies at the University of Alberta. Her research interests include using hermeneutic phenomenological methodology to examine the pedagogical significance of computer-technology tools in the classroom.

Robyn Barnacle is a senior research fellow in the Graduate Research Office at RMIT University, Melbourne. She teaches in the area of research education and her main research activities focus on research practice and knowledge generation; research education, including pedagogy, practice and policy; and ontology and learning.

Michael Bonnett, formerly Senior Lecturer in the Philosophy of Education at the University of Cambridge, is currently Reader in Philosophy of Education at the University of Bath and Senior Research Fellow at the University of London Institute of Education. He is the author of the books *Children's Thinking* (1994) and *Retrieving Nature: Education for a Post-Humanist Age* (2004). His current interests are in the philosophical exploration of issues arising from environmental concern, the philosophical implications of information technology for education, and the constitution of subjective identities and the nature and importance of self-knowledge in education.

Angus Brook is a lecturer in philosophy at the University of Notre Dame, Australia on the Sydney campus. His main interests are phenomenology, philosophy of religion, ontology, and ethics.

Gloria Dall'Alba teaches and researches in the area of teaching and learning in higher education in the School of Education at the University of Queensland in Brisbane, Australia. She has a particular interest in professional education and questions of research methodology. Her work draws upon hermeneutic phenomenology, especially relating to notions of learning, teaching, professional practice, and inquiry. Her recent book is entitled *Learning to be Professionals* (2009).

Lisa C. Ehrich is a senior lecturer in the School of Learning & Professional Studies at Queensland University of Technology in Brisbane, Australia. She teaches in the under-graduate Bachelor of Adult and Community Learning degree and Masters of Learning Innovation program. Her substantive research interests lie in the field of educational leadership, phenomenology, and mentoring for professionals.

Krishnaveni Ganeson is a teacher in the Human, Society and its Environment Faculty at Asquith Girls' High School in New South Wales, Australia. She teaches economics, business studies, and business services in the senior school, and commerce and geography in the junior school.

Michael A. Peters is Professor of Education at the University of Illinois at Urbana-Champaign. He has degrees in geography, philosophy and education. He previously held a chair as research professor and professor of education at the University of Glasgow (2000–2005) as well as a personal chair at the University of Auckland and adjunct professor of communication studies at the Auckland University of Technology. He is the editor of three international journals: Educational Philosophy and Theory; Policy Futures in Education; and E-Learning. He is also the author or editor of over forty books, including most recently *Global Knowledge Cultures* (2007), *Knowledge Economy, Development and the Future of Higher Education* (2007), *Building Knowledge Cultures: Education in the Age of Knowledge Capitalism* (2006), and *Deconstructing Derrida: Tasks for the New Humanities* (2005). His research interests include educational philosophy, education and public policy, social and political theory.

Max van Manen is a professor of education at the University of Alberta, Canada. He teaches phenomenology and human science research methods, pedagogy and curriculum studies. His books include *The Tact of Teaching* (1991), *Researching Lived Experience* (1997), and *Writing in the Dark* (2002).

Foreword: Heidegger, Phenomenology, Education

> The time of 'systems' is over. The time of re-building the essential shaping of beings according to the truth of be-ing has not yet arrived. In the meantime, in crossing to an other beginning, philosophy has to have achieved one crucial thing: projecting-open, i.e., the grounding enopening of the free-play of the time-space of the truth of be-ing. How is this one thing to be accomplished? (Heidegger, 1999: 4)

Phenomenology has had a significant impact in the history of modern Western philosophy beginning perhaps with Husserl and developed in different ways by Heidegger before being taken up by a range of thinkers that have shaped philosophy, sociology and anthropology in the modern era. The movement began with Husserl's *Logische Untersuchungen* (1900–1901) which was a fierce attack on psychologism. Phenomenology studies the structure of consciousness as it is experienced from the first person perspective, focusing on the central characteristic of intentionality. Various forms of existential and hermeneutical phenomenology can be traced back to Heidegger and his project of fundamental ontology influencing a wide range of thinkers including Jean-Paul Sartre, Simone de Beauvoir, Maurice Merleau-Ponty, Henri Lefebvre, Paul Ricoeur, Patrick Heelan, Don Ihde, Calvin O. Schrag, and Gianni Vattimo.

Heidegger and his forms of phenomenology have been a neglected figure in the field of philosophy of education in the English-speaking world. Little has been written on Heidegger or about his work and its significance for educational thought and practice. This is, perhaps, surprising given the recent upsurge of interest in his work by philosophers in the English-speaking world and, in particular, the way his thought is a source of inspiration to contemporary French and German philosophy, especially those movements which we know as 'poststructuralism' and hermeneutics. There are a number of possible reasons for this relative degree of neglect: first, his work is deemed to be too complex and English-speaking philosophers of education, accordingly, have been discouraged from reading his notoriously neologised texts; second, ever since Carnap's attack upon Heidegger's metaphysics, analytic philosophers have been 'taught' or conditioned to despise him for his 'opacity' and 'nonsense', even though Heidegger's professed aim is to move beyond metaphysics, and; third, Heidegger's association with and support for the Nazis' cause during the year of his rectorship at Freiburg and after, have rightly offended many scholars and had the consequence of making Heidegger both a risky and unappealing figure in which to intellectually invest, until very recently.[1]

Gilbert Ryle (1929: 370) was among the first to review Heidegger's *Being and Time*, and while Ryle was critical of aspects of his thought, at the same time he approved of Heidegger's general project, describing him as a 'thinker of real importance' who with 'immense subtlety' and 'originality' 'tries to think beyond the stock categories of orthodox philosophy and psychology'. After Ryle's early engagement we had to wait over 50 years in the English-speaking world before Heidegger became acceptable to read and the first commentaries began to appear. Charles Guignon (1993) records the recent upsurge of interest in the English-speaking world, especially in the influential writings of Richard Rorty (1991), Charles Taylor (1985) and Hubert Dreyfus (1991), who together have increased our appreciation of Heidegger as 'one of the greatest thinkers of our time' (p. 1)—a thinker who has contributed to the 'hermeneutical turn' (Hoy, 1993) in philosophy, humanities and human sciences.

Yet given this relative neglect, as I have argued previously (Peters, 2002) I think a convincing argument can be made for the centrality of his philosophy to education including Heidegger's critique of the ontotheological tradition, his interpretation of Nietzsche's work, together with his overriding concern for the question of the meaning of Being. Heidegger's notion of 'authenticity' and his influence upon French thinkers, especially Jean-Paul Sartre's existentialism make an interesting story from the phenomenological perspective of the educational subject. Heidegger's influence on education might be traced indirectly through his impact on phenomenology, hermeneutics and existentialism, as theoretical approaches in education considered as a social science, but also in terms of his influence upon the development of modern psychiatry, psycho-therapy and school counselling.

Heidegger's approach to 'the question concerning technology' and modern science—his critique of forms of rationalism and instrumentalism—are essential to understanding modern and increasingly highly-technologized forms of education. Yet most obviously, Heidegger's critique of the 'false anthropologism' of humanism is central to understanding humanistic education in the West, insofar as humanism has always been based upon an educational ideal.

Many of his texts, especially those works that come to us as *lectures* he gave to specific audiences, are specifically and self-consciously *pedagogical*, and that Heidegger was explicitly concerned with pedagogical matters, as is well evidenced his discussion of 'learning' in *What is Called Thinking?* Heidegger (1968: 3) begins his course of lectures—a set of twenty-one lectures—which he delivers to his students during 1951 and 1952, with the following words: 'We come to know what it means to think when we ourselves try to think. If the attempt is to be successful, we must be ready to learn thinking.' Learning, in other words, is central to understanding thinking. He continues: 'In order to be capable of thinking, we need to learn it first. What is learning? Man learns when he disposes everything he does to him at any given moment. We learn to think by giving our mind to what there is to think about' (p. 4). Yet he suggests while there is an interest in philosophy there is no 'readiness' to think. The fact is that, even though we live in the most thought-provoking age 'we are still not thinking' (p. 4). In *What is Called Thinking?* Heidegger is concerned with 'learning' and construes the learner on the model of the apprentice, emphasizing the notion of 'relatedness'—of the cabinetmaker's apprentice to the different kinds of wood that sustain the craft. The 'relatedness' of the learner-apprentice to his craft or subject, he determines will depend on the presence of a teacher. Heidegger writes:

> Teaching is even more difficult than learning. We know that; but we rarely think about it. And why is teaching more difficult than learning? Not because the teacher must have a larger store of information, and have it always ready. Teaching is more difficult than learning because what teaching call for is this: to let learn. The real teacher, in fact, lets nothing else be learned than—learning. (p. 15)

J. Glen Gray (1968: vi) helps to clarify the importance of learning and teaching to Heidegger by drawing attention to the fact that the lectures which constitute *What is Called Thinking?* were the first course of public lectures Heidegger was permitted to give by the French occupying powers since 1944, the point at which the Nazis drafted him into the people's militia. Gray (1968: vi) explains:

> What this long interruption in his teaching activity must have cost him is not difficult to guess, for Heidegger is above all else a teacher. It is no accident that nearly all his publications since *Being and Time* (1927) were first lectures or seminar discussions. For him the spoken word is greatly superior to the written, as it was for Plato. In his book he names Socrates, a teacher not an author, 'the purest thinker of the West'.

No philosopher since Socrates, was so committed to questions of education and to good teaching as Heidegger. As he indicates the metaphor of the *path* or the *way* (*weg*) has been the guiding principle of his thought, just as it is for education. Education for Heidegger constitutes a passage into thought that involves our entire being. Heidegger focuses on the essence of his entire philosophy and rests his career upon a way or a path he first took on writing *Being and Time* (1927). Heidegger through his work talks of the *way* (*weg*), the way of thinking, of learning, of questioning. As he says in the Preface to the German edition of *Pathmarks* (Heidegger, 1998: xiii), published in German under the title *Wegmarken*, 'This volume of already published texts ... seeks to bring to attention something of the path that shows itself to thinking only on the way: shows itself and withdraws'. It is a path leading to the *vocation* of thinking but it bring nothing new, leading us only to before the oldest of the old. He adds:

> Whoever attempts to start out on this path is helped only by the unceasing endeavor to locate by discussion (to find at its locale) what the word 'being' once revealed as something to be thought, what it may once perhaps conceal as something thought. Whoever sets out on the path of thinking knows least of all concerning the matter that ... determines his vocation and moves him toward it. Whoever lets himself enter upon the way toward an abode in the oldest of the old will bow to the necessity of later being understood differently than he thought he understood himself. (p. xiii)

In *Contributions to Philosophy (From Enowning)* (Heidegger, 1999: 3), widely regarded as his second major work, Heidegger begins:

> *Contributions to Philosophy* enact a questioning along a pathway which is first traced out by the crossing to the other beginning, into which Western thinking is now entering. This pathway brings the crossing into the openness of history and establishes the crossing as perhaps a very long sojourn, in the enactment of which the other beginning of thinking always remains only an intimation, though already decisive.

I make this point through exegesis of Heidegger's writings because it helps explain his approach to the question of being and to a kind of thinking that is outside metaphysics. It also indicates how Heidegger holds to a notion of thought, thinking and language that is somehow outside the control of Man, something that once embarked upon has its own natural trajectory. In a sense, Heidegger believes that his thinking is a pathway that has its own contours and direction, which he must follow, if he is to follow the way.

The crossroads is also the historic crossroads of the trivium (grammar, rhetoric, and dialectic), which defined the medieval university. The trivium, properly means three subjects pursued separately and already contains within itself a multiplicity— *tri-via-ium*, three-roads made into one. Heidegger pursues each of the three ways, grammar, dialectic and rhetoric, one by one. If I provide only a gloss of Heidegger philosophy it is because his thought is complex and consists in returning to the original underlying Latin and Greek concepts, the puns and metaphors that suffuse these subjects. The trivium must be linked to ethics and the question of being in a pedagogy that grows out of his fundamental ontology. The grammar of being, foreshadowed in the Latin 'case', is a falling away, just as fallenness of Dasein understood as relatedness to everyday things, is our first condition and authentic existence is concerned with the question of where the path we tread is leading.

Echoing the temporality of case (in grammar) and the object-subject relation built into language, Heidegger suggests that the pedagogical relation between teacher and student is understood in homologous terms: The teacher gives *eidos*, form and finality, to the student as spiritual material presented for shaping and forming *kata ton logon*, in accordance with an abstract model. Heidegger looks to Aristotle for an interpretation that avoids the 'productionist metaphysics' constituting pedagogy understood by analogy with *techne*.[2] By contrast, this is a pedagogy understood by analogy with *physis*, where '*morphe* is to be paired with self-creating and self-emerging *physis* rather than with technical *hyle*, the raw matter of production'. Following an Aristotelian metaphor Heidegger intimates that education is inextricably bound to the meaning of being with the result that the university emerges as a clearing in which the relation between teacher and student takes on different shapes and forms.

It is in respect of rhetoric that Heidegger most firmly links his view of pedagogy and education to his developed philosophy. It is rhetoric, he says, that both deserves and stands in need of legitmation. In *Being and Time*, he remarks that he began to rethink the traditional correspondence theory of truth in terms of figuration. By contrast, Heidegger designates truth as *aletheia*, as concrete truth as world disclosure, a concept that does not efface difference and accentuate identity in order to prevail.

Heidegger stood for election as the Rector of Frieburg University in late 1932 and was elected to office in April 1933, whereupon he joined the Nazi Party. He remained Rector until resigning in April 1934. During his time as Rector he did away with the University's democratic structures and made a number of public speeches where he advocated loyalty to the Party and the *Führer* principle, establishing himself as a virtual dictator and introducing Nazi 'cleansing laws' to the students body ending financial aid for all 'non-Aryans'. It is also alleged that during this time he acted as a Nazi informer, secretly denouncing Jewish colleagues (Sheenan, 1993: 86–7). He continued to support the Nazi regime even after he resigned from the rectorate in April 1934 although not uncritically. By 1936, Charles Guignon (1993: 32) claims that Heidegger was pulling back from direct involvement in Nazi politics. He suggests that Heidegger's initial substitution of the *Volk* for the individual—the spiritual mission of the German *Volk* as a nationalist ideology transmuting *Dasein*—begins to ebb in Heidegger's work as he struggles to come to terms with the domination of Western metaphysics by subjectivism and humanism.[3]

Heidegger's rehabilitation of rhetoric as a forerunner of new ways of world disclosure that puts the trope on a cognitive par with intuition and inference bespeaks simultaneously of the grounding of Heidegger's pedagogy in early Greek philosophy, its attachment to his own philosophy of being, and his historical attempt to distance himself from Nazi ideology. Yet for a philosophy that was once adduced to the Nazi cause and interpreted as a world-historical moment delivering the German people and Europe from the worst excesses of modernization, one at least has to raise a doubt about the apparent ease with which the same philosophy, in the spirit of self-correction, can retrospectively cast pedagogy as part of the primordial fullness of being that existed in the pre-Socratics.

In the quotation from *Contributions* with which I began Heidegger writes of the end of 'systems' and the beginning of the openness and truth of being. This remark and those around it constitute a profound consideration on the nature of being and its relation in education to the growing movement of openness (open source, open access, open publishing) which is still yet a consequence of systems and distributed knowledge but that offers ontologically the means for becoming open: being open and open being.

Notes

1. The next few paragraphs are drawn from my Introduction in Peters (2002).
2. We must remember that Heidegger's remarks concerning *techne* here pre-date the essay 'The Question Concerning Technology' which provides a fuller exposition of the role of *techne* in relation to being and introduces the concept of the technological enframing of being in the modern period.
3. There has been an on-going debate about Heidegger's involvement with the Nazi cause, which intensified after the publication of Victor Farias's (1987) *Heidegger and Nazism*. On the question of whether Heidegger's politics were an intrinsic part of his philosophy see Young (1997).

References

Couzens Hoy, D. (1993) Heidegger and the Hermeneutic Turn, in: C. B. Guignon (ed.), *The Cambridge Companion to Heidegger* (Cambridge, Cambridge University Press).

Dreyfus, H. (1991) *Being-in-the-World: A Commentary on Heidegger's Being and Time, Division I* (Cambridge, Mass. London, MIT Press).

Guignon, C. (1993) Introduction, in: C. Guignon (ed.), *The Cambridge Companion to Heidegger* (Cambridge, Cambridge University Press), pp. 1–41.

Heidegger, M. (1968) *What is Called Thinking?* (New York, Harper & Row).

Heidegger, M. (1977) *The Question Concerning Technology, And Other Essays*, trans. and with an introd. W. Lovitt (New York, Garland Pub).

Heidegger, M. (1979) *Heraclitus Seminar, 1966/67*, M. Heidegger and E. Fink, trans. C. H. Seibert (University, Ala., University of Alabama Press).

Heidegger, M. (1985) The Self-Affirmation of the German University, together with The Rectorate 1933/34: Facts and Thoughts, *Review of Metaphysics*, 38 (March): 467–502.

Heidegger, M. (1999) *Contributions to Philosophy (From Enowning)*, trans. P. Emad & K. Maly (Bloomington & Indianapolis, Indiana University Press).

Peters, M. A. (2000) Heidegger, Derrida, and the New Humanities, in: G. Biesta and D. Egea-Kuehne (eds), *Derrida and Education* (London, Routledge).

Peters, M. A. (2002) (ed.) *Heidegger, Education and Modernity* (Lanham, Boulder, CA, Rowman and Littlefield).

Rorty, R. (1991) *Essays on Heidegger and Others: Philosophical Papers, Volume 2* (Cambridge, Cambridge University Press).

Ryle, G. (1929) Review of Heidegger's *Sein und Zeit*, *Mind*. Collected Papers Volume 1, Critical Essays. Edited J. Tanney (Routledge, 2009).

Taylor, C. (1985) Interpretation & the Sciences of Man in *Philosophical Papers 2* (Cambridge, Cambridge University Press).

Taylor, C. (1995) Heidegger, Language, Ecology in *Philosophical Arguments* (Cambridge, M. Harvard Univesity Press).

Young, J. (1997) *Heidegger, Philosophy, Nazism* (Cambridge, Cambridge University Press).

1

Introduction to Diverse Approaches to Phenomenology and Education

GLORIA DALL'ALBA

Increasing interest in phenomenology as a philosophy and a research movement among educationalists, as well as in some other areas of the humanities and social sciences, makes this book both timely and relevant for educational debate. There is no doubting the extensive influence of phenomenologists such as Edmund Husserl, Martin Heidegger, Hanna Arendt, Maurice Merleau-Ponty, Hans-Georg Gadamer, Jean-Paul Sartre and Alfred Schutz on research and scholarship in philosophy, where phenomenology has its origins. As the impact of phenomenology extended beyond philosophy to fields such as sociology, education, anthropology, politics, linguistics, psychology and feminist studies, it has challenged taken-for-granted assumptions and prompted new insights into what it means to live, work, play and learn in our world. This interest in phenomenology can perhaps be understood in the context of its potential contribution to re-thinking our understanding of the complex phenomena we encounter in the dynamic and, at times, confronting world in which we find ourselves in this 21st century.

Not surprisingly, this book on phenomenology and education is rich in its diversity and breadth. This is as it should be, especially as the chapters do not have in common a specific educational question or issue as their focus. Instead, in their different ways, the authors explore contributions of phenomenology to educational practice and research, demonstrating phenomenology is a contemporary movement that is both dynamic and varied (see also Spiegelberg, 1982). In addition, some of the chapters bring phenomenology into dialogue with other research approaches, such as feminist scholarship. This again reflects the development of thought and scholarship in contemporary phenomenology, whereby phenomenology is enriched by other research approaches while also making a substantial contribution to them.

The refereed chapters in this book address a range of key educational issues including learning through the body, writing online, being an authentic teacher, ambiguities in becoming professionals, schools as places that disturb the self, and school transition. The chapters are equally varied in the theories and concepts upon which they draw. Through interrogating ideas from phenomenology, this book provides insights into a range of educational questions. In addition to insights into specific questions, the chapters illustrate a range of ways of inquiring phenomenologically. Martin Heidegger (1962/1927), Maurice Merleau-Ponty (1962/1945), Hans-Georg Gadamer (1989/1960) and others have argued that phenomenology is not a method but a 'way of inquiring' that must be responsive to the phenomena being explored. This emphasis is consistent with Edmund Husserl's call to 'return to the things themselves', a central tenet of the various branches of phenomenology.

A clear demonstration of a way of 'doing phenomenology', or inquiring phenomenologically, can be seen in the chapter by Max van Manen and Cathy Adams. In their evocative chapter they explore various aspects of writing online, with rich use of metaphor. Given the increasingly pervasive use of online environments across educational settings, Max van Manen and Cathy Adams' chapter makes a pertinent and timely contribution to understanding learning and teaching online.

While Max van Manen and Cathy Adams incorporate embodiment when they explore writing online, Robyn Barnacle makes the body and learning the focus of her chapter. She adopts a phenomenological approach to recent feminist scholarship that challenges a neglect of biology in accounts of the body and mind-body relations, using the role played by the gut to illustrate the arguments. She considers implications of re-thinking mind-body relations for learning. Robyn Barnacle's chapter stretches the boundaries of the way we typically think about learning in educational settings.

Michael Bonnett's chapter also casts new light on learning in educational settings. He thoughtfully explores the question of whether schools can be places in which the self can be disturbed—in both positive and negative ways. More particularly, he poses a question about whether these disturbances can be pathological for students to the extent their potential for selfhood is diminished. The chapter by Michael Bonnett prompts us to think about educational institutions in new ways, especially in terms of the kinds of places that schools are for students.

Two of the remaining chapters address issues related to becoming professionals, including teachers in schools. My own chapter explores learning during professional education programs, where I argue for the need to reconfigure these programs as a process of becoming that is always open and incomplete. Martin Heidegger's phenomenology of education forms a background for the chapter, while Maurice Merleau-Ponty's concept of 'ambiguity' provides a means of exploring how professional ways of being can be learned. The chapter has relevance for all those who contribute to professional education programs, as well as continuing education.

In Angus Brook's chapter, he describes his own experience of attempting to use Martin Heidegger's phenomenology in coming to terms with becoming a teacher. He explores what authenticity means in teaching and learning, with a view to investigating ways in which phenomenology can inform teaching practice. He touches on a theme taken up in my own chapter when he explores teaching and learning in terms of students' becoming. Angus Brook's chapter is located in the transition from writing a PhD thesis on Heideggerian phenomenology to becoming a school teacher. It provides a form of pragmatic validity (Kvale, 1989) for key concepts, such as authenticity, through testing their relevance and applicability to challenges in the practice of teaching.

The chapter by Lisa Ehrich and Krishnaveni Ganeson is also about transition. It reports an empirical study that explores students' experiences of transition to high school, which for large numbers of school students coincides with the early years of adolescence. Using the phenomenological psychological approach developed by Amedeo Giorgi, they identify important aspects of school transition, confirming as well as calling into question previous research on school transition and middle schooling. They discuss implications for facilitating the transition to high school that have the potential to benefit new high school students and schools.

This book shows how insights into key educational questions can be achieved through exploring and interrogating ideas and concepts from phenomenology, as well as through inquiring phenomenologically. It demonstrates ways in which phenomenology can inform a broad range of aspects of educational theorising and practice. My hope is that the book will form part of a critical and constructive dialogue on the contribution that phenomenology can continue to make to educational practice and research.

References

Gadamer, H. G. (1989/1960) *Truth and Method* 2nd revised edn., trans. revised by J. Weinsheimer & D. Marshall (New York, Crossroad).

Heidegger, M. (1962/1927) *Being and Time,* trans. J. Macquarrie & E. Robinson (New York, SCM Press).

Kvale, S. (1989) To validate is to Question, in S. Kvale (ed.) *Issues of Validity in Qualitative Research* (Lund, Studentlitteratur), pp. 73–91.

Merleau-Ponty, M. (1962/1945) *Phenomenology of Perception,* trans. C. Smith (London, Routledge & Kegan Paul).

Spiegelberg, H. (1982) *The Phenomenological Movement* 3rd revised edn. (The Hague, Martinus Nijhoff).

2

The Phenomenology of Space in Writing Online

MAX VAN MANEN & CATHERINE ADAMS

In recent years, college and university teachers have been increasingly required to integrate technology in their teaching, and institutions schedule ever more courses online. Especially in postgraduate programs there is a preponderance of alternative online offerings whereby much of the interaction is through reading and writing texts. Students encounter their teacher, other students, and their subject matter through words on the screen. Literally, the text and the computer screen are the media that mediate the pedagogical relations and educational experiences. In this chapter, the phenomenology of writing is explored to study the phenomenon of space: nearness and distance, proximity and relationality in online writing.

Are the changes of the new writing technologies significant for the text itself? Over a century ago, Nietzsche, inspired by his new typewriter, wrote, 'Our writing instruments contribute to our thoughts'.[1] Typewriting, and more particularly writing with keyboard and mouse, changes how we write, and the way our words look as we write. But how do the writing instruments contribute to our (writing) thoughts? Jacques Derrida, the philosopher of writing, was hesitant: 'People often ask me, "Has your writing changed since you have been writing on the computer?" I'm incapable of replying. I don't know what criteria to measure it by. There's certainly a change but I'm not sure that it affects what is written ...' (2005, p. 25). Indeed, it would be difficult to measure how a text might have looked differently if the handwritten manuscript was compared to the version prepared by means of digital keyboard. Of course, the pen or pencil is also a writing technology though much 'simpler' than the black box of the computer. And the keyboard involves the hands and fingers no less intensely (but much differently) than writing a text with ballpoint or pen and ink. Here we want to examine what may be observed about the new technologies of writing and especially how temporal and dimensional place and space are experienced differently in writing online.

Probably few authors (in countries rich with modern technological resources) still write exclusively with pen and paper. People who regularly engage in narrative, poetic, or reflective writing tend to use the computer. Further, the once stand-alone computer with word processor is increasingly 'wired', and thus maintains a virtually unbroken connection to the global network. In other words, contemporary writing may be described as 'writing online.' This does not necessarily mean that writers are immediately sharing their work on the Internet, but the place shaped by the networked computer is now only a click away from the publishing space of the Web. In fact, some varieties of word processing software are now supported online while writing in the private space of one's personal computer.

Thus arises the question: Is this new kind of writing by means of online technologies affected in a manner that differs significantly from the technology of the pen on paper, the typewriter, or the word processor in an off-line environment? To be sure many of us still partake in handwriting, such as when we take notes, try out some thoughts, or keep track of ideas that occur to us while we do not have a keyboard at hand. And, therefore, we can measure our own experiences against the reflections on the question of the phenomenology of writing online. In this chapter, we first evoke some general features of the experience of writing. Next we turn to the question of writing online and the space of writing. Does writing online open up a different sense of space from earlier forms of writing. We examine the phenomenon of online writing, not only to contribute to our understanding of online writing, but ultimately to contribute to a more pedagogically sensitive understanding of teaching and learning online.

Where Are We When We Write?

Where are we when we write? We may look at our present space: this office space in the home, this coffee shop, this desk, this kitchen table. This is where we may feel we work best. 'This is where I write.' So is this then the space of writing? Yes and no. When we are actually writing, scribbling on a piece of paper, typing on a keyboard, or writing mentally while staring into space, then we seem to be somewhere else. So, where are we then? We might answer: 'Inside my thoughts.' The writer dwells in an inner space, inside the self. Indeed this is a popular way of spatially envisioning the self: an inner self and an outer self. But phenomenologically it is just as plausible to say that the writer dwells in the space that the words open up.

The physiology of writing is not unlike reading a story. To read a story, we have to find a space that is good for reading this or that book, fictional or nonfictional. It must be a space that is comfortable for the body, but not too comfortable. It does not need to be quiet as long as the sounds or people do not draw attention to themselves. Some people may be able to read in spaces where others cannot. But many would probably agree that some places are more amenable to reading than others. In a phenomenological sense, we may notice that even this physical space is already multi-aspectual. We have to make the physical space our own by positioning ourselves bodily, and mentally too, claiming a certain privacy. Then we have to claim a certain temporal space as well. We need an undisturbed space of time where we can dwell in the timelessness of the space of reading.

Once we have found this phenomenological space conducive to reading or writing, we are ready, so to speak, to enter that other space, the space opened by the words that transports us away from our everyday reality to the reality of the text. When we have entered this world of the text then we are somewhere else. So it seems that the physical space of reading or writing allows us to pass through it into the world opened up by the words, the space of the text. The actions of picking up a book, opening it, and sitting down to read it, or turning on the computer, opening a blank document, and beginning to type, all involve the body orienting itself in physical space. But this space includes more than bodily movements. The sense of space constantly seems to shift in the transitions of picking up a book to read, or in opening the text document on the screen. There are spatial aspects even to the graphic nature of the letters we produce: letters written with a pen or pencil possess a certain substantiality in terms of the ink or graphite that is deposited on the paper. But digital writing involves a less substantial and more ethereal form of sedimentation.

But is this not a misleading way of speaking? After all, the space opened up by the text is not physical dimensional space. Is the idea of textual space not just a metaphor and therefore a gloss for how we actually experience the process of reading and writing? This seems to be true. We are using a spatial-temporal phenomenology. But the term *space* itself possesses rich semantic meanings. Etymologically space does not just refer to physical extension and perspective. The term *space* also possesses the meaning of lapse or duration in time. It refers both to the time and the three-dimensional field of everyday existence.

Space carries the meaning of temporal and physical expanse as well as the time spent in an experience. When we open up a book or when we open a new page on our word processor and we enter the perspectival space of the text we enjoy a temporal experience of opening ourselves to, and an opening of, the world evoked by the words of the text. Perhaps the experiential meaning of the space of the text lies in this 'opening' that we seek but never quite find.

Writing Public

Some of us still remember how it was when entire papers were written exclusively 'by hand'—scrawled, crossed-out, scribbled, with numbered pages, notes in the margins, pencilled arrows and occasional taped-on sections. Only the final draft would be laboriously and carefully typed (and sometimes retyped). And too, we may recall the first time we ever used a word-processor to write. Having typed just a few sentences, perhaps using the delete key or even the mouse to make a change, we may have sat back amazed. Suddenly, with these magic tools, the words verily invited us to edit them, to try out new possibilities. At the same time, the text already 'looked' so perfect, so clean, so published.

The handwritten text, littered with the traces and evidence of past editing, preserved a certain intimacy, closeness, and scarred imperfection. We may even remember which of the editing we performed in the coffee shop, on the bus, or late one night. Perhaps only we could decipher some of the illegible insertions and notes needed for the next draft of the text. In contrast, the word-processed text seems to have lost some of this intimacy and the reminders of the time and place where we scrawled some additional sentences or phrases into the text. The text that emerges from writing online constantly looks perfect already (though we may know it needs more editing). At any moment it has already lost the scars of the editing we may have performed only seconds ago. The online written text looks both familiar ('I know I wrote this!') and distant ('Did I write this?').

Too, typing or keyboarding removes the handwritten word of its personal and idiosyncratic qualities, visual uniqueness. It casts text in the presentable type-face of public font. On the screen, authored words stare back at their writer in a new and unexpected way. They are strikingly clean, professional and 'published' but still remain supple, open and unfinished. In this online writing space, words seem to invite rather than resist revision and authorship. At the same time, ambiguously, the words already appear perfect and finished, near ready for publication.

In the paper-and-ink days, the editing evidence of our writing was right there in the waste paper basket filled to the brim with crumpled up paper. Nowadays the messiness of our writing is temporarily saved as a history of undo-redo moves accessible through the edit menu, or is simply removed with a stroke of a button. But finally, when the deadline is upon us, or the text seems done (however incomplete or imperfect) we have to let go of it. From now on it will lead a life of its own. It will constitute a textorium, a space for others to enter—to gaze at what may reveal itself. But what is this life? Online, a text may continue to waver indefinitely, never settling on a final, 'published' state. In a wikispace, for example, a text can change without notice from its original, having been edited, rewritten or even entirely obliterated by another writer. In a journal database, our words persist unchanged, mimicking the constancy of printed text. In yet another online environment, we may suddenly find our words made public in an unexpected, unintended way, and irretrievably lost to our reach or recourse.

Once published, whether online or off-line, a text does seem to have a life of its own in another sense. It is other; it is not dependent on its author or its reader, or even on some external reference to which the text points. This condition is known as the autonomy of the text and an entire hermeneutic of reading and critical semiotics has been built on the notion of textual autonomy and authority (Barthes, 1977; Foucault, 1977).

As authors, we may feel sometimes that our written text is misinterpreted or over-interpreted. We may regret a thoughtless phrase. We may wish that we had not sent a letter or email, that we had not published a premature manuscript. Once a text is in the public space, it is often beyond our control. There exist obvious political and personal implications in this autonomous life of the text that we create. Furthermore, a written text can make a plea for its own immortality, in spite of its author's intentions. The ease and speed with which our writing can be emailed or posted online, may deceive us into 'forgetting' that it may never ever be retrievable. The uncomplicated invitation to revise, the already 'done' appearance of digital text, and the immediate access to the online publishing domain, may each serve to subvert the resistance of thoughtful reflection, once experienced in the insistent wait inherent in traditional writing technologies and publishing procedures.

The moment of writing is consequential and differs from the moment of speaking in that we can rewrite while we write. In rewriting we can try to weigh our words: we can check their semantic values, we can clarify their meanings, we can taste their tonalities, we can measure their effects on the imagined reader, we can explicate and then try to bracket our assumptions, and we can compose and recompose our language and come back to the text again and again to get it hopefully 'just right', drawing meaning from the dark.

From an originating point of view, the spoken word is irrevocable in a manner that is rarely true of the written word. In a normal conversation or discussion, what has been said and heard cannot be taken back. Of course, we can apologize for some things that may have slipped our tongue. We may try to deny that we said what has been heard. We may correct ourselves, and say what it is that we 'really meant to say'. We may add meaning through a certain tone of voice or physiognomic expression. We may repeat or paraphrase our earlier points when we feel that we are being misunderstood or when we feel that our words do not seem to have their intended or hoped-for effect. And yet, what has been heard has been heard; and, therefore, what we say can never be completely revoked. Indeed, our spoken words some day may be brought back to us, to remind us of things we may wish forgotten. All this is equally true, but complicated in the absence of the pathic nuances and context of in-person conversation, when our words are electronically recorded and dispersed into the well-greased public information space of the Web.

Cyberwriting

When we talk of cyberspace, digital landscapes, or the electronic frontier, what place or places are we referring to? When we connect to the Internet, are we *in* some space, cyberspace? Consider how Bruce Sterling, a cyberpunk writer and theoretician, describes cyberspace as 'the place between', a vibrant, but insubstantial world sprung out of the thin, dark conversational space of the telephone:

> Cyberspace is the 'place' where a telephone conversation appears to occur. Not inside your actual phone, the plastic device on your desk. Not inside the other person's phone, in some other city. *The place between* the phones ... [I]n the past twenty years, this electrical 'space', which was once thin and dark and one-dimensional—little more than a narrow speaking-tube, stretching from phone to phone—has flung itself open like a gigantic jack-in-the-box. Light has flooded upon it, the eerie light of the glowing computer screen. This dark electric netherworld has become a vast flowering electronic landscape. (1992, ¶2, 4)

But what does it mean to speak of cyberspace in terms of the mythical language of the netherworld? Sterling suggests that cyberspace is a multi-modal technetronic place where computers connect in digital space or the place where telephone conversations occur. Cyberspace elicits images of empty space, other realities, dark regions beyond our sensory reach. But, the nature of the conversational space of face-to-face relations is ultimately as elusive as the conversational space of the telephone. It is neither in the telephone set nor on the tongue or in the mouth, neither in the cables nor in the audible waves of the air separating people involved in a conversation.

What then is the space that we enter when we read or write online? This 'dark electric netherworld' of which Sterling writes is strongly reminiscent of the dark Orphean underworld that Maurice Blanchot evokes in his portrayals of the space of literature in which the writer dwells. Whereas, Sterling uses the metaphor of a dark netherworld to arrive at a conceptualization of cyberspace, Blanchot involves us in more serious philosophical reflection of the nature of this dark underworld of the space of the text where writing occurs.

Blanchot, who has reflected perhaps more patiently and more deeply than any other philosopher on the nature and experience of writing, insistently returns to the theme of coming to the realization of the illusionary nature of the real. Blanchot uses the allegory of Orpheus to allude to what happens in the act of writing (1982, pp. 171–176). The story of Orpheus, son of Apollo and the muse Calliope, is well known. It happened that shortly after their marriage Orpheus' wife Eurydice dies from the poison of a snake bite. The grieving Orpheus descends into the dark caverns of the underworld to implore the gods with his songs to reunite him with Eurydice and allow him to take her back to the daylight world of the living. This is a classic story about the power of the artist. Orpheus enchants the ferryman Charon, the hellish three-headed dog Cerberus, and the monstrous Erinyes. His songs are so moving and so stirring of the soul that finally, Hades and Persephone grant his wish to take Eurydice with him from the realm of the dead, but on one condition: that he will not turn around to look at her till they should have reached the upper air of daylight (Bulfinch, 1981).

They proceed in total silence, he leading and she following, through passages dark and steep, till they nearly reach the cheerful and bright upper world. Just then, it is said, in a moment of forgetfulness, as if to assure himself that she was still following him, Orpheus casts a glance behind. At that very instant she is borne away. Eurydice is snatched from him so fast that their stretched-out hands for a last embrace, fail to reach each other. Orpheus grasps only the air, and her last words of farewell recede with such speed that they barely reach his ears. He has lost her for a second time and now this loss is forever. All that Orpheus is left with is the image of that fleeting gaze that he saw of Eurydice. This is the way the story is usually told: 'when in fear he might again lose her, and anxious for another look at her, he turned his eyes so he could gaze upon her' (Ovid, 95–98). But the philosopher Blanchot (1982) suggests a different interpretation: Orpheus was not forgetful at all. He was motivated by a different gaze: the gaze of desire.

According to Blanchot the ambiguous gaze of Orpheus was no accident. He does not subscribe to the romantic view according to which Orpheus tragically forgot the promise he made in a moment of anxious unguardedness. The gaze was motivated by desire, says Blanchot. But it was not the simple desire for the person, Eurydice, in her visible flesh and blood appearance. No, says Blanchot, Orpheus 'does not want Eurydice in her daytime truth and her everyday appeal, but [he] wants her in her nocturnal obscurity, in her distance, with her closed body and sealed face—[he] wants to see her not when she is visible, but when she is invisible, and not as the intimacy of a familiar life, but as the foreignness of what excludes all intimacy' (1982, p. 172).

What Orpheus came to seek in the darkness of the Underworld was not a lost love, but the hidden meaning of love itself. 'That alone is what Orpheus came to seek in the Underworld,' says Blanchot. He came 'to look in the night at what night hides' (1982, p. 172). It is about a mortal gaining a vision of what is essentially invisible, the perfection of Eurydice—before she resumed her mortal state as they approached the light of day.

Love had driven Orpheus into the dark. His consuming desire was to 'see' and to 'feel its form.' But such glance is not permitted to mortals. What lies on the other side belongs to the great silence, to a 'night' that is not human. So the gaze of Orpheus expresses a desire that can never be completely fulfilled: to see the true being of something. And yet it is this veil of the dark that every writer tries to penetrate. This is the very nature of writing, Blanchot explains, 'Writing begins with Orpheus's gaze' (1982, p. 176). And one writes only, if one has entered that space under the influence of the gaze. Or perhaps it is the gaze that opens the space of writing. As Blanchot says so eloquently, 'When Orpheus descends toward Eurydice, art is the power by which night opens' (1982, p. 171).

The writer uses words to uncover a truth that seems almost within reach. And indeed, at first it seems that Orpheus's words (his poetic songs) bring his love into presence. His words and songs have made her visible, so to speak. He dimly discerns the image of his love in the dark of the Underworld. But this is not enough. He desires to see more clearly. He must bring her back from the dark of night to the light of day. Orpheus is not satisfied with the image evoked by his words. He wants the immediacy of a presence—a presence that is not mediated by words or other means. This is a presence that is not some-thing or some-one evoked, but an evocation nevertheless. Orpheus turns around and gazes at Eurydice. He wants to see the invisible in the visible. And for that reason he must turn around twice—paradoxically he must turn away from her to see her: away from Eurydice (into the dark of the Underworld through which he must find his way) and towards Eurydice (to see her in her immortality). In his desire, Orpheus turns away from his love to see Love. He must turn his gaze toward the image in the space of the text that he tries to grasp in his writing, and he glances towards Eurydice who he desires to see in her perfection of Love itself.

So what does Orpheus see? Love in its primal appearance? A mere image? In this writerly wondering gaze one may hope to see existence in its nude appearance, peer past the veneer of human constructs. How is this possible? Does such realm exist? The writer can find the answer to this question in the experience of writing itself, in the virtuality of the text where one may run up against the human wall of language or where one may be permitted a momentary gaze through its crevices. It is striking how Blanchot's likening of the Orphean underworld with the space of the text is evocative also of the contemporary images of cyberspace.

Blanchot suggests that Orpheus' supposed 'mistake' in looking back was actually a determined deed, just as the writer wilfully peers into the dark of the text to discern a human 'truth' that can be beautiful but also frightening. Orpheus' journey up through the dark passages of the underworld can indeed be likened to the difficult traversing of the shadowy space of the text where we can be confronted with reality realizations that are more real than life itself. But what do we make of mistakes? 'Mistakes' in the more fluid processes of online writing are perhaps less wilful and sometimes more expressive of subterranean and contingent phantoms that make us substitute one word with a more or less fortuitous term, reshape a phrase, or accidentally delete a line, at the whim or measured click of the mouse.

Writing the Distance to the Other

In online text spaces—discussion-boards, email, blogs—we come to know the other through writing alone. Relation is not perturbed or infected by visuality or orality, physical presence or vocal discourse. We do not meet the other's eyes; rather, we read and are read by the other's text. We move and are moved by word alone. Online, we have no access or visceral response to the pre-reflective, tacit understandings of another's bodily being, voice and gesture, smell and presence. We come to know the other through a single modality: text. Here, textuality is the sole interstitial site of meaning, presence, contact, and touch.

Otherness is felt in the particular choice of words, in the style and tone of writerly presence, in the manner participants respond (or not) to others online. All else is left to the imagination. In this way, writing online forces us into a mode of pure relation. We sense the other through their text. We are touched by and desire to touch the other through the text we write. Once we have met a person face-to-face and we know their gestures, we will read their text differently. The text will now be read against the carnal qualities that make up this person. The body is written back onto the text as it were, and the text rewrites the face-to-face relation. And yet author and embodied person may remain strangely incommensurable. Even when online interaction is combined with facial images, text and face may still be difficult to reconcile.

How is responding online (writing on a web discussion board) different from responding orally (speaking up) in a seminar class? We obviously tend to experience the space of speaking differently than the space of writing. In face-to-face situations speaking and hearing are more likely conversationally and relationally intertwined. The speaker speaks in a listening way and the listener listens in a speaking manner. Even monologues (lectures, speeches, addresses) tend to have this conversational spatial quality in the sense that speakers may tend to focus on particular individuals in the audience with whom they feel conversationally connected. People who have a talk together tend to be more intimately tied into the relational space than people who are listening to a lecture. Conversations involve the interchange of personal interiors, says Walter Ong (1986, p. 167). That is why it makes such important difference whether a lecture is delivered *ad lib* (retaining a conversational relational quality) or whether it is largely read from prepared script.

Conversational relational space has a certain quality of immediacy. In normal discussions we are physically immediately present to the other person's speaking. The telephone, too, retains a sense of this immediacy. This temporal-spatial immediacy also means that the speaker cannot erase what has been said. One cannot restart a conversation in the way that one can restart a written text. One cannot edit out a phrase and replace it with a more appropriate one. One cannot step back reflectively from one's spoken word to monitor and adjust the effects that selected words and phrases seem to exercise on other words we utter. In contrast, the space of writing has a different and more reflective temporal-spatial quality. Yet this quality may be compromised and transformed through the new technologies of online writing. Compared to handwriting, the temporality of online environments speeds writing up dramatically: as soon as we type it, it is already there, perhaps even corrected. The whole experience of editing, writing, editing follows much closer to our train of thought; it has the immediacy of conversation.

One may begin to write with someone in mind, for whom or to whom one writes. But when one starts to write then other(s) may disappear. As we continue writing we may get caught up in the words and then absorbed in the mood-space of writing and gradually it seems that we are addressing no-one (not one). Or perhaps, the writer is the one, inhabiting a textual space of one. 'I do not think that I have written for anyone at all,' says Helene Cixous. 'This does not mean that I scorn the reader, quite the contrary, ... But I do not know who it is. I only know there is one. (But who?)' (1997, p. 100).

In writing a poem—for example, a love poem—writing seems to somehow destroy and recreate the other person at the same time. In contrast, when we are engaged in a real eye-to-eye conversation with someone then we do not seem to lose ourselves in the space of text in that same way. The other person looks at us, touches us with his or her eyes, and so we experience a certain togetherness that we may not experience when writing.

Some authors have commented on the intensely solitary dimension of writing. In the moment of writing I am here by myself at this writing desk and in this writing space. But I am also with myself, the first reader is the self: the first other is oneself. As one writes it may happen that the space opened by the text becomes charged with a signification that is, in effect, more real than real. As readers, many of us know this phenomenon. Many readers have at one time or another been profoundly moved in the realization of being touched by a human insight. And this insight might not have affected us this deeply if we had undergone the experience in the sober light of day, rather than in the realm of the novel, story, or poem. 'Reading a text oralizes it,' says Ong (1982, p. 175). This accounts for the strange sensation of immediacy of presence that a vocative text can induce (see Steiner, 1989).

There is something paradoxical about the un-reality of a powerful text: it can be experienced by the writer or reader as real, as unreally real, as nearer than the nearness that things may have in ordinary reality. This super reality turns the insights we gain in the space of the text essentially virtual, unencumbered by the presence of all the other memories, impressions, and factualities that permeate the affairs of our everyday life.

The moment we at last begin to write, we surrender to the silent space of the text, and allow ourselves to be embraced by time's absence. But before this timeless, intimate expanse opens, we must in some sense be summoned. Such tyrannical prehension (Blanchot, 1982, p. 25), the insistent demand to write *right now*, is perhaps more rarely than regularly experienced by writers. Yet, can we not see in this wakeful moment the desirous force that opens every piece of writing? To write, to put hands to keyboard and make perceptible the inchoate speech pressing, is to yield to this demand.

Entering the Page: Proximity and Distance

Sometimes the space of writing seems to open with the simple gesture of putting fingers to keyboard and beginning to type. But is it really so easy to begin? For Blanchot (1982), 'one writes only if one reaches the instant which nevertheless one can only approach in the space opened by the movement of writing. To write, one must write already.' (p. 176). This impossible contradiction haunts the start of many writing projects. There is no magic beginning, no sure method, no guarantee that entering a fresh page will take us to the other side. Blanchot speaks of the darkness of the space of text since the writer (and the reader) has to leave the ordinary everyday world of daylight and sight to enter it. Phenomenologically the writer faces darkness also in trying to see what cannot really be seen. As Robert Frost once said: writing is 'like falling forward into the dark.' Here meanings resonate and reverberate with reflective being.

While writing on the computer increasingly replaces writing on paper, the page we open on the desktop perfectly mimics the page of a paper or a book. And yet, there are obvious differences. Whereas the paper page occupies physical space, the virtual page of the word processor is like its phantom image: shimmery and somehow untouchable. The new page on a word processor is like a paper page, but even more so: innocent but also treacherous. Margaret Atwood (1998) warns the would-be writer not to approach 'the page that waits' too lightly.

> If you decide to enter the page, take a knife and some matches, and something that will roar. Take something you can hold onto, and a prism to split the light and a talisman that works, which should be hung on a chain around your neck: that's for getting back. It doesn't matter what kind of shoes, but your hands should be bare. You should never go into the page with gloves on. Such decisions, needless to say, should not be made lightly.
>
> There are those, of course, who enter the page without deciding, without meaning to. Some of these have charmed lives and no difficulty, but most never make it out at all. For them the page appears as a well, a lovely pool in which they catch sight of a face, their own but better. These unfortunates do not jump: rather they fall, and the page closes over their heads without a sound, without a seam, and is immediately as whole and empty, as glassy, as enticing as before. (1998, p. 56)

The virtual page of the computer screen may be even more inviting and dangerously depthful than the paper page that lies in front of us on the desk. Once the writing begins, the words draw us in. Whether we are writing on bright white paper or digitized screen, we are in the dark, in a state of unknowing, a kind of agony.

What is familiar has become strange. Yet, in the dark, feeling our way, we may suddenly happen upon something familiar. That something is recognized because it has been 'seen,' perhaps without any significance, many times before in the daylight. But in the darkness of the space of the text, it attains new significance for it is now grasped in a very different modality. Like Orpheus traversing the dark underworld in search of his beloved Eurydice, our nocturnal wanderings may reveal truth experiences that daylight is unwilling or unable to yield to us.

Writing Revisited

Writing aims to engage; the writer is charged with using words to draw the reader (and indeed the writer him- or herself) closer and 'into' the text itself, to render living experience immediately sensible, near and recognizable. The person who learns to 'really' write, gains the experience of being in touch with something. One writes to make contact, to achieve intimacy with a human insight, a 'truth.' But the moment when the writer senses that contact (close in-touchness) has been achieved, something strange may happen: it appears that this contact came from the outside. Rather than touching something with words, the writer feels being touched, an invitation as it were. The touch says: 'Come!' But the *jouissance* of online writing may draw us into a deeper mystery: we recognize something unrecognizable.

Even as our text seems to draw us nearer to the contact we desire, it inevitably retains its elusive, veiled distance. The text that fascinates touches 'in immediate proximity; it seizes and ceaselessly draws [us] close, even though it leaves [us] absolutely at a distance' (Blanchot, 1982, p. 32). As more and more online courses are mediated by the practice of 'writing' online, what we provocatively call 'real writing' seems to have become both easier and more difficult. Writing is not the practice of some clever technique or the setting in motion of a word processor; neither is writing restricted to the moment where one sets pen to paper, or fingers to the keyboard. Writing has already begun, so to speak, when one has managed to enter the space of the text, the textorium. Online computer technologies intensify the phenomenology of writing—they speed up, accelerate, compel, draw us into the virtual vortex of the experience of writing—while simultaneously raising questions about the potential loss of reflectivity, the unaccustomed yet easy publicness of publishing to the Web, and the uncharted complexity of human relation through text.

Note

1. Kittler (1990), translates this from a footnote of a typed letter from Friedrich Nietzsche to Peter Gast, dated February 1882, found in *Briefwechsel*, ed. Elisabeth Förster-Nietzsche and Peter Gast (Berlin-Leipzig 1902–09), IV, p. 97.

References

Atwood, M. (1998) *Murder in the Dark: Short Fiction and prose poems* (Toronto, McClelland & Stewart).

Barthes, R. (1977) The Death of the Author, in: S. Heath (ed.), *Image-music-text: Roland Barthes* (London, Hill and Wang), pp. 142–148.

Blanchot, M. (1982) *The Space of Literature* (Lincoln, University of Nebraska Press).

Bulfinch, T. (1981) *Myths of Greece and Rome* (New York, Penguin).

Cixous, H. (1997) *Rootprints: Memory and life writing. Helene Cixous and Mireille Calle-Gruber* (London, Routledge).

Derrida, J. (2005) *Paper Machine* (Stanford, CA, Stanford University Press).

Foucault, M. (1977) What is an Author?, in: D. F. Bouchard (ed.), *Language, Counter Memory, Practice* (Ithaca, NY, Cornell University Press), pp. 113–138.

Kittler, F. (1990) The Mechanized Philosopher, in: L. A. Rickels (ed.), *Looking After Nietzsche* (Albany, State University of New York Press), pp. 195–207.

Ong, W. J. (1982) *Orality and Literacy: The technologizing of the word* (London, Methuen).

Ong, W. J. (1986) *The Presence of the Word* (Minneapolis, The University of Minnesota Press).

Steiner, G. (1989) *Real Presences* (Chicago, The University of Chicago Press).

Sterling, B. (1992) *The Hacker Crackdown* (Introduction). Retrieved 20 August, 2006 from <http://www.mit.edu/hacker/introduction.html>

3
Gut Instinct: The body and learning

ROBYN BARNACLE

Introduction

At one level the role of the body in learning is obvious: one needs a body in order to experience the world. The old 'brain in the vat' scenario is untenable. All too often, however, such conceptions of the role of the body conceal a particular ontology in which the body is treated as 'housing' the brain and mind, which tend to get viewed as co-extensive. This container view of mind-body relations is widespread, both within everyday conceptions and academic ones (and I have commented on it in detail elsewhere, see Dall'Alba & Barnacle, 2007). Moreover, it is reinforced by the rationalistic tendencies of contemporary educational discourse and practice. Performance-based funding and quality control, managerialism, and an overwhelming concern with efficiency, are all hallmarks of contemporary universities. These, in turn, promote rationalistic pedagogies that foreground educational content and approaches amenable to quantification and itemization. Learning then becomes increasingly understood in terms of metrics: a process, in other words, of accumulation and acquisition of discrete knowledge objects, skills and competencies.

Whilst demands for measurability may make rationalistic characterisations of learning appealing, just how well do they describe the learning process? More specifically, what aspects of learning does rationalism overlook? Rationalistic conceptions of learning presume a model of the subject characterised by a rational mind presiding, hierarchically, over an inert body. Embodiment is not considered epistemologically important. But can sensibility and perception really be dismissed so easily? Recent feminist scholarship is demonstrating that attending to physiology can open up new ways of understanding the various ways in which embodiment conditions everyday being-in-the-world. Recent phenomenological inquiries into cognition and the body support this. My question is: what implications do these insights have for how embodiment is understood, and, by extension, learning? How do informal, non-cognitive modes of knowing, or of engaging with the world, inform learning in higher education contexts? More specifically, what role do non-cognitive modes of engagement, such as sensibility, have in augmenting, enabling or delimiting the learning process?

Feminist Turn

The body has tended to have a pejorative status within western thought. This is due, not in small part, to an ongoing association with the female gender, and this has in turn led to an interest in the subject amongst feminist scholars. One key aspect of this has been a critique of the way in which western thought has failed to recognise, in Elizabeth Grosz's words, 'the excluded term *body* as the *unacknowledged condition* of the dominant term, *reason*' (1995, p. 32). In other words, feminist scholars have argued that the dominance of reason in accounts of what it means to be human, the nature of knowledge, etc., systematically deny the body and, at the same time, fail to come to terms with a necessary dependence on embodiment. Feminists have therefore foregrounded the problematical status of the body and sought to re-think its status and role. As educators, engaged in the transmission and generation of knowledge, this critique has obvious relevance.

But inquiry into the body is not without its challenges. While discourse on the body continues to proliferate within and beyond feminist inquiry, the body itself is rarely afforded more than a very limited agency. A number of feminist scholars, particularly, Vicki Kirby (1997), Karen Barad (2003), and Elizabeth Wilson (2004a,b) have been challenging this. They question why the interest in the body within feminist theory has not been extended to the physiological or neurological body. The reasons for avoiding such matters are not without basis, centring as they do on concerns with the possible implications of biological reduction to a feminist politics. For Kirby, Barad and Wilson, however, the fact that such concerns have led to a curtailment of a whole domain of inquiry is problematic. Feminist inquiries into embodiment have focused on the cultural construction of the body to the exclusion of inquiries into the biological itself. For Wilson:

> Too often, it is only when anatomy or physiology or biochemistry are removed from the analytic scene (or, in what amounts to much the same gesture, these domains are considered to be too reductive to be analytically interesting) that it has been possible to generate a recognizably feminist account of the body. (2004b, p. 70)

This one-sidedness is mistaken, claims Kirby, Barad and Wilson, for, amongst other things, it perpetuates a conception of mind-body relations that should be cause for concern. This is the conception that has dominated western thinking since Descartes, where thought and the symbolic are treated as reigning over the biological and material more broadly. It is through a re-engagement with the biological that these feminist scholars hope to offer a more distributed, less hierarchical conception of mind-body relations.

Psyche and Soma

Wilson argues (2004a,b) that in order to understand the current status of the biological within feminist theory one must attend to Sigmund Freud's legacy and, in particular, a truncation that occurred in his early clinical approach. This truncation would resonate for years to come, according to Wilson, in the way in which inquiry in the humanities and social sciences has dealt with the body and embodiment generally. Originally, Freud focused his research interests on two key modalities of the body: the neurological and the psychological, and undertook clinical studies related to each. In the late nineteenth century, however, a transition was made in which analysis of neurology ceased and Freud focused solely on psychology. Wilson argues that this was to have a profound impact on the trajectory of future feminist scholarship in that it enabled it, too, '... to think bodily transformation ideationally and symbolically, without reference to biological constraints' (2004b, p. 69). If the psychological and neurological can be disassociated then it becomes possible to, as Wilson puts it, '... think about the body as if anatomy did not exist' (2004b, p. 69). Throughout the 1980s and 1990s feminist scholars examined gender issues through an analysis of how psychological or cultural conflicts could become somatic events, in the form of hysteria, for example. The model, borrowed from Freud, in which psychological and ideational effects could be considered without reference to biology—neurology, for example—meant that it was possible to consider embodiment as if a fundamental demarcation exists between the psyche and soma. Moreover, in a demarcation such as this, the symbolic and psychological are privileged while physiology, and physiological conditions, are treated as subject to the effects of psychology, and the symbolic more broadly, but not the other way around.

While much of Wilson's work concerns itself with a level of clinical detail beyond the scope of this chapter, her call to feminist scholars to engage with neurobiological data has the potential to open-up new ways of understanding embodiment with implications across the humanities and social sciences: '... exploring the entanglement of biochemistry, affectivity, and the physiology of the internal organs will provide us with new avenues into the body' (2004b, p. 14). Her analysis of neurology, in particular, demonstrates the extent to which a failure to engage with biological level data has resulted in an acceptance of models that reinforce rather than question established hierarchies, for example, '... the tendency to equate the central nervous system with cognition—desexualised, calculating, and autocratic' (2004b, p. 29). By drawing on clinical data from Freud and others Wilson shows how hierarchical models which situate the central nervous system and cognition above and in control of the so called lower functions of the enteric nervous system cannot account for what actually occurs in both bodily and psychological processes and events. Challenging what is seen as an overwhelming focus within psychoanalysis on the central nervous system, Wilson provides examples from clinical studies that demonstrate why one needs to look beyond the central nervous system and head to understand the relation between psyche and body. 'The nervous system extends well beyond the skull, and as it so travels through the body it takes the psyche with it' (2004b, p. 47).

One site of this interaction that interests Wilson is the gut. The gut, like the psychological sphere, interacts directly with the outside world: the former in the formation of relations with others, and through that the self, and the latter as a canal that passes all the way through the body, from mouth to anus, in the ingestion, digestion and excretion of food. The gut is actually an exterior passage through the body, allowing the outside world to literally pass right through us. The role of the gut in mediating between inside and outside parallels that of the psyche. But whereas we think of the psyche as dynamically involved in the development and maintenance of one's relations with others and the world, the gut rarely gets attributed such a role. As Wilson points out, however, Freud recognised from his earliest studies that close links exist between digestion and psychology, manifesting in disorders such as anorexia, depression etc. This leads Wilson to argue that the gut, in that it, like the psyche, is intimately attuned to the outside world, is '... a vital organ in the maintenance of relations to others' (2004b, p. 45). The link between mood and appetite has long been recognised, but this has usually been understood in terms of the effect of the psyche on the gut, rather than the gut itself responding to a failure to connect with others, for example, as in depression. The internalization of relations with others is predominantly understood as something that occurs within the psyche, and so, by extension, within one's head, in which any bodily effects are considered secondary expressions. It is this hierarchy of relations between central and peripheral nervous system, psyche and soma, which Wilson seeks to challenge. For example, it may come as a surprise to some to learn that the gut contains 95% of the body's serotonin (see Wilson, 2004a). This is the chemical that Prozac and other antidepressants act on in an attempt to normalise mood. For Wilson:

> The large stocks of serotonin in the gut, the morphological similarities between gut neurons and brain neurons, and the clearly psychological character of gut function all suggest that it is not just ideation that is disrupted in depression; it is also the gut. (2004b, p. 45)

The import of Wilson's analysis is that the gut is itself capable of complex emotional responses. In other words, it can get depressed too, as well as angry, excited, anxious and serene.

> The gut is sometimes angry, sometimes depressed, sometimes acutely self-destructive; under the stress of severe dieting, these inclinations come to dominate the gut's responsivity to the world. At these moments any radical distinction between stomach and mood, between vomiting and rage is artificial. (2004a, p. 84)

It is interesting to note that recognition of the emotionality of the gut is evident in everyday expressions, such as gutless, which refers to a lack of courage, or a fearful gut. In addition, both the notions of 'gut reaction' and 'gut instinct' treat the gut as a site of specific responsiveness to the world, the former in an immediate, unreflective sort of way, and the latter, conversely, as a particularly fine-tuned and insightful form of intelligence. In addition, both conceptions attribute autonomy to the gut. This sees it operating independently from the seat of so-called 'higher order' intelligence: the brain. Indeed, it is partly due to this perceived autonomy that we tend to treat our gut instincts as offering real insight and our gut reactions as expressing what we really feel or think.

Whilst we have merely touched on the complex issues raised by Wilson in an area of inquiry that she also recognises as nascent, Wilson's analysis of the psychology of the gut offers the beginnings of an alternative account of the role of physiology within mind-body relations. Analyses of this kind have the potential to change the way that we think about embodiment. Might this also have a bearing on how we understand learning and knowing?

Embodiment and Knowing

I have been exploring the role of embodiment in knowing with colleague Gloria Dall'Alba for the last few years (see: Dall'Alba & Barnacle, 2005, 2007). We have sought to challenge traditional accounts of what it means to learn and know by developing an integrated account of knowing, acting and being. This integrative account seeks to address and encompass the whole person, thereby challenging the narrow, intellect centred, conception of learning that has tended to dominate pedagogical models, particularly within higher education. In doing this we have argued for a privileging of ontological rather than epistemological conceptions and issues. One of the challenges of such a project, however, is that of how to engage with the body as such and, in particular, adequately account for the complexity of mind-body relations. As sketched above, humanities scholars have tended to engage with the body through the symbolic and the social, cultural and historical construction of gender. In our own work, Dall'Alba and I have recognised the tensions involved in making proclamations about embodiment which, without providing evidence for how embodiment conditions everyday being in the world, become little more than assertions. As Kirby, Barad and Wilson also note, the body can be strangely absent from its accounts. In challenging this, however, by re-engaging with biology, there is a need to proceed with caution. Interest in the role of biology in learning has been abused in the past. The eugenics movement is a case in point, which relied on a reductive account of biology, particularly genetic inheritance, to account for intelligence, amongst other things (Greer, 1984). However, attending to the biological in mind-body relations need not lead to such crude reductionisms. On the contrary, it can offer insight into the complexity of being in the world, and the challenges of adequately accounting for it as a phenomenon.

The question of how being in the world can be explained or understood is, of course, highly contested. This is reflected in the ongoing debate within cognitive science and phenomenological inquiry on the role and status of each to the other (see Gallagher, 2002). The reductiveness of cognitive science has been seen by phenomenologists as a barrier to understanding the complexity of embodiment while cognitive scientists, such as Daniel Dennett, have been dismissive of phenomenology for what is mistakenly considered to be its introspectiveness. According to Shaun Gallagher, however, each has something to offer the other in understanding embodiment. Neuroscientific analysis offers insight into the physical or objective body while phenomenology offers insight into the lived body—or the condition of being embodied. By drawing on both, Gallagher provides an account of the role of the body in cognition, drawing specifically on developmental studies that show: '... *how* embodiment provides certain innate capacities that enable and condition our experience of ourselves and others' (2002).

The Body and Cognition

Drawing on studies of infant and pre-natal development, Gallagher argues not only that a capacity for self-consciousness exists prior to birth, but that such a capacity is neither conceptual nor linguistic in that it instead emerges through embodiment. This primitive, non-conceptual, embodied form of self-consciousness manifests in a first person sense of bodily agency and control (that I am moving and am the one causing the movement); a pragmatic differentiation between self and non-self; and recognition that an other person is the same sort as oneself.

Gallagher's insights are of interest because they suggest that embodiment and self-consciousness not only go hand in hand but that embodiment is essential to a very primitive, or fundamental, form of learning: the development of a sense of self and other. In the Cartesian era, self-consciousness tends to be regarded as co-extensive with thought: 'I think, therefore I am'. In Gallagher's alternative formulation, however, one's sense of being is engendered through a primitive bodily awareness that has little to do with thought, in the conceptual sense. In other words, the innate capacities that Gallagher refers to develop prior to birth, and so are already active prior to entering into the Cartesian symbolic realm.

These insights into the role of the body in cognition suggest an account of mind-body relations in which biology is not simply offering the 'hardware' for thought, in the form of a brain, and a nervous system for transmitting sensory input. Instead, the intricate relation between mind and body that forms embodiment seems to offer much more: the condition for the possibility of self-consciousness. Without this, any 'hardware' or 'software' would be redundant.

As stated above, my work with Dall'Alba has explored a model of learning that integrates knowing, acting and being. How mind-body relations are understood will have a considerable impact on the way in which such a notion is conceived as well as its realisation in practice. If education is to address, engage, and transform the whole person, of relevance is the question of how the subject is constituted: whether vertically, through the dominance of the brain, central nervous system and intellect, or in a more distributed fashion.

Gallagher and Wilson both offer insight into mind-body relations. Whilst Wilson shows how psyche and soma resist demarcation at a fundamental level, Gallagher suggests how embodiment can be understood as the seat of self-consciousness. In both accounts, developing and sustaining one's sense of self in relation to others is not merely or even primarily a cerebral phenomenon.

It is worth reflecting for a moment on why a preference for everything cerebral might have come to dominate both conceptions of the Western subject and the role and purpose of education. Historically, what is prized about the brain—and why it is privileged over every other organ in the body—is its capacity to reason. And it is not just hard-nosed pragmatism (its capacity to get us out of trouble, for example) that has made reason so prized. Two historical thinkers whose solutions to the so-called problem of the body have been profoundly influential are Descartes and St Augustine. While for the former the solution was a primarily secular one and the latter theological, both sought redemption from the effects of embodiment. For each embodiment is traumatic: Descartes because of the deceptiveness of sensory experience and St Augustine because of the corruptibility of the passions. For both, reason is privileged due to its capacity to provide self-control, critical analysis etc. (although both ultimately rely on some degree of divine intervention to resolve their respective issues. For Descartes, for example, it is God who ensures man is connected to the world).

In seeking to re-engage mind-body relations it is important not to lose sight of why the body was considered a problem in the first place, particularly if we are to avoid merely reversing established hierarchies. What is interesting about the insights offered by Gallagher and Wilson is that they provide a way of re-thinking mind-body relations that complicates rather than erases demarcation between the two. Difference needs to be thought without the absolute or fundamental character it has been conferred in the past. Most of us, at the end of the day, would like to think we can call on our capacity for reason to direct us in times of difficulty rather than rely on gut reaction alone. What is needed, therefore, is an understanding of mind-body relations that preserves difference whilst at the same time, as Kirby says, engages the complex and distributed nature of that difference:

> Instead of mind *and* body, the conjunction that assumes that difference happens at *one* interface, *between* entities, we might think the body as myriad interfacings, infinite partitionings—as a field of transformational, regenerative splittings, and differings ... (Kirby, 1997, p. 148)

Learning between the Biological and Symbolic

Although neither Gallagher nor Wilson addresses the issue of learning, it seems to me that there are educational implications arising from their work. Both point to a mode of engagement with the world that seems to occur between the biological and symbolic, in that it is reducible to neither but is related to both.

This has resonances with an account of learning offered by the phenomenologist Hubert Dreyfus (2006). He discusses a form of learning that emerges in the context of both the natural and the constituted in that it is neither biologically nor symbolically determined. This is the learning that occurs in the establishment of what Dreyfus calls social norms, or practices, which inform social interactions. One such interaction is that which occurs when determining how close to stand in front of someone when speaking: the jostling that can occur between two people as they each seek out a comfortable space for discourse. Dreyfus distinguishes the social norms that are negotiated in this sort of occasion from more established institutional rules, or what he calls facts. Institutional rules act like facts because they are governed by an over-riding symbolic order that imposes apparently inflexible meaning designators on persons, practices and things. Rules or facts of this kind have become institutionalised through collective agreement; they are the agreed cultural rules that a society collectively bestows on the world, and are therefore contingent to that society. Dreyfus uses the example of gender. Certain physical features are associated with each gender, and the rules, rights and obligations that govern each gender are made explicit and codified within a given culture. It is not that such rules are unbreakable but that a member of a given culture knows what they are because they are established and reinforced. According to Dreyfus, institutional rules differ from social norms by the degree of codification. Social norms are not learnt or transmitted through codified rules, but instead, through negotiation, or in Dreyfus' words, by: '... acquiring a sense of what is collectively considered appropriate and inappropriate' (2006). Acquiring a sense of how to behave is qualitatively different to knowing and applying established rules of behaviour within a given circumstance. In the case of determining how close to stand in front of someone while speaking, for example, that sense is gained when interlocutors find a comfortable 'fit' through mutual jostling, rather than through the application of a set of rules. It is this difference that interests Dreyfus in that whereas institutionalised rules are governed by propositional knowledge, social norms are not.

According to Dreyfus, the key difference between these two modes in which social reality is constructed and negotiated is that whereas institutional rules are reproduced through linguistic representation, learning social norms does not require linguistic mediation. For Dreyfus:

> It turns out that there are cases in which ... a prelinguistic sense of tension can create a sense of the appropriateness and inappropriateness of a social activity without the mediation of linguistic representations. (2006)

Through this account of how social norms are developed, acquired and transmitted, Dreyfus provides a case of learning that is reducible neither to pure biology—or automatic neuronal mechanisms—nor cognitive states. This is significant because it undermines the dominance of the mental—whether conceived as experience or states—in the formation of meaning and understanding. Instead, such learning could be described as a kind of 'embodied practice', to borrow from Gallagher (2005), in that it is non-conceptual, involving the emotions, sensory-motor responses and perception. In a similar vein to Dreyfus, Gallagher argues that: '... these embodied practices constitute our primary access for understanding others ...' (2005, p. 224). Indeed, for Dreyfus, the mode of engagement with others that occurs in the negotiation of social norms itself provides the basis for the more formal, conceptual, mode of engagement characteristic of the deployment of propositional knowledge. What Dreyfus calls 'embodied intentionality' forms the basis of all propositional knowledge in that it is the driver for the establishment of new forms of understanding. Crucially, then, not only are formal and embodied knowing integrated but the former is dependent on the latter.

Implications for Education

The learning occasion described by Dreyfus in the development of social norms is informal but clearly has implications for formal learning occasions as well. It follows from his account that all forms of learning participate in an embodied form of knowing, in the sense that all knowing is necessarily embodied. Dreyfus' conception recalls Maurice Merleau-Ponty (1962, 1998) and in particular his claim that 'I am my body', or in other words, that we are body-subjects, unable to detach mind from body, subject from object, etc. For Merleau-Ponty, our embodied state of being means that the symbolic or ideational is inextricably linked to the material and biological because each is relationally constituted. Both Dreyfus' and Gallagher's accounts of embodiment suggest that pre-symbolic, embodied practices provide a primary mode of access to others and the world. Wilson shows how the physiological and psychological mutually inform each other, including one's sense of self and relation to others. The body-subject that emerges from these accounts is an integrated or incorporated self, to borrow from Michael O'Donovan-Anderson (1996), to which the container model of mind-body relations just cannot do justice. Indeed, these accounts offer an alternative to abstract notions of selfhood in that a sense or intimation of self and of being in the world becomes a pre-condition for conceptual understanding more broadly rather than the other way around (a conception that finds broad support in the phenomenological literature, see Martin Heidegger (1993/1978), for example).

What are the implications of this for formal educational contexts such as universities? As educators, we are used to the idea of promoting 'the life of the mind', but what about the idea of promoting 'the life of the gut'? If the gut is actively engaged with the world, psychologically, then how does this influence the way that we think, what we think about, and what we do?

One aspect of the gut that could be examined in relation to learning is its role in orienting thought. By this I mean that aspect of thinking that involves attraction and repulsion: the orientation of thought toward and away from certain topics, ideas, etc. If the gut is a site in which engagement can be particularly resonant, how do its intensities function within formal educational contexts? Do such contexts foster and promote these intensities? Are they even recognised? For example, is the gut's role in moderating mood or generating emotional responses something that can be harnessed or utilized, particularly in regards to arousing interest in a topic, for example? My aim in foregrounding this dimension of thought is not merely to point out the obvious—that our interests are not only or simply directed by processes of rational decision-making—but to ask how this recognition can be used to inform educational practices.

One specific way in which the gut could be understood as informing thinking processes and educational choices is through intimations and hunches: sense making. If having a sense of something prefigures conceptualisation, as Dreyfus argues, then it follows that teaching and learning practices that attend directly to sense making could assist in the learning process. This would mean promoting learning situations in which a sense of what is being learnt, or more accurately, a sensibility for what is being learnt, is actively cultivated along with the development of more formal or intellectual understanding. Doctoral candidates, for example, need to develop a sense of what their thesis is all about well before they are ready to articulate it in a single pithy statement. It is this sense—only partially formed and intimated—that propels them. Moreover, for any degree program, promoting a sensibility for the way in which a discipline engages with the world is one of the key, although often unexpressed, purposes of the curriculum.

Indeed, these less tangible aspects of thought do not currently go entirely unrecognised. Hunches and instincts are widely recognised in the conduct of research suggesting that sense making is an integral aspect of knowledge generation at the highest level. It is necessarily the case, for example, that if inquiry is to create new knowledge it must move beyond existing knowledge, and therefore, a received set of concepts, ideas and practices. This requires the mobilisation of sensibility in concert with intellect. Moreover, thought of this kind that is precarious in that it dabbles beyond the given, is not insignificant within formal education either. It is central, for example, to the development of independent and critical thinking. These so-called 'generic capabilities' are currently highly prized for their supposed transferability into the workplace. And yet, is learning critical thinking an acquirable skill in the way quality assurance regimes suppose? Browse any library catalogue on critical thinking and you will find an overwhelming dominance of books on informal logic. Critical thinking, it is often presumed, is a skill grounded primarily in reasoning ability. This has been challenged on a number of fronts, through the claim, for example, that subject knowledge plays a greater role in critical thinking than reasoning (see McPeck, 1981). Perhaps even more crucial to critical thinking ability, however, is something far less tangible: personal qualities and dispositions, such as openness and a commitment to seek the truth. It is highly questionable, however, that such qualities and dispositions can be taught through direct instruction at all. In addition, as Nigel Blake *et al.* (2000) point out, the notion of skill is inadequate for describing what a quality such as openness involves. Qualities and dispositions are sensibilities and, as such, address and involve one's whole approach to life. Being critical, therefore, becomes an aspect of how one lives one's life, and this is not reducible to a specific skill set that can be deployed or withheld at will. A gut, engaged 'moodfully' with the world, to borrow from Heidegger, offers a better model for describing such a phenomenon than a conception of mind dominated by a calculating brain.

While the idea that informal modes of learning and knowing are operative in everyday and formal learning contexts is not new, the extent to which they are recognised or harnessed is unclear. The tangibility of formal knowledge makes it amenable to quantification—ever popular in this age of quality control—and thus, it tends to occupy the centre of attention. As Heidegger recognised, the logic of efficiency has a persuasiveness the rational mind struggles to reject. In other words, if we want to challenge rationalism we need to promote other ways of being-in-the-world. Indeed, it is perhaps in regards to this point where engaging the gut in learning could also be considered relevant to advancing a feminist agenda. Educational approaches that address the role of the body in learning problematise rationalism, and therefore, challenge dominant accounts of knowledge, being in the world, etc.

In advancing the case for recognition of informal modes of knowing in learning, however, we also need to be wary of only telling one side of the story. The role of the gut in the psyche, as Freud recognised, is not always benign. Sensibilities can orient thought in ways not necessarily beneficial and can also limit or truncate one's openness to inquiry. Hunches need not be right. Moreover, sensibilities are open to manipulation and can mask or stand in for undisclosed or unrecognised prejudices, biases etc. As an operative condition within thought, sensibilities, hunches, and instincts necessarily inform how we approach learning and inquiry, and as such, deserve our attention.

That some scholars within education are beginning to move in this direction and attend to the broader, less tangible, dimensions of learning is already evident in the literature. There is a growing awareness that learning must attend ultimately not only to the intellect but the whole person, and therefore, to transforming who we are as people (Barnett, 2004, 2005). From the skills debate, for example, Mary Kalantzis and Bill Martin argue for a conception of learning:

> ... which is less about imparting defined knowledge and skills and more about shaping a kind of person: somebody who knows what they don't know; knows how to learn what they need to know; knows how to create knowledge through problem solving; knows how to create knowledge by drawing on informational and human resources around them; knows how to make knowledge collaboratively; knows how to nurture, mentor, and teach others; and knows how to document and pass on personal knowledge. (2006)

The ideas explored in this chapter can assist efforts to account for the kind of knowing called on above by re-thinking the central role that reason has traditionally been accorded in accounts of learning and understanding. Such efforts can also be progressed by scholars looking beyond the traditional borders of humanities and social science research, or that which encompasses culture and the symbolic, to improve understanding of biological processes and events and the role that they might play in learning. By recognising the arbitrariness of the bifurcation of the world into the natural and non-natural there is the possibility for new paths of educational inquiry and, ultimately, improved educational approaches and outcomes.

Acknowledgement

This chapter has seen various iterations and has gradually evolved based on the feedback received. I would particularly like to thank the anonymous reviewers of this chapter for their suggestions as well as participants in the symposium on phenomenology in education at the European Conference on Educational Research, Geneva 2006.

References

Barad, K. (2003) Posthumanist Performativity: Toward an understanding of how matter comes to matter, *Signs*, 28, pp. 801–831.

Barnett, R. (2004) Learning for an Unknown Future, *Higher Education Research and Development*, 23:3, pp. 247–260.

Barnett, R. (2005) Recapturing the Universal in the University, *Educational Philosophy and Theory*, 37, pp. 785–797.

Blake, N., Smeyers, P., Smith, R. & Standish, P. (2000) *Education in an Age of Nihilism* (London, Routledge Falmer).

Dall'Alba, G. & Barnacle, R. (2005) Embodied Knowing in Online Environments, *Educational Philosophy and Theory*, 37:7, pp. 719–744.

Dall'Alba, G. & Barnacle, R. (2007) An Ontological Turn for Higher Education, *Studies in Higher Education*, 32:6, pp. 679–691.

Dreyfus, H. (2006) *A Phenomenology of Skill Acquisition as the Basis for a Merleau-Pontian Non-Representationalist Cognitive Science*. Retrieved July 2006 at: http://ist-socrates.berkeley.edu/~hdreyfus/html/papers.html

Gallagher, S. (2002) *Phenomenological and Experimental Research on Embodied Experience*. Paper presented at Phénoménologie et Cognition Research Group, Centre de Recherche en Epistémologie Appliquée (CREA), Ecole Polytechnique, Paris (December 2000). Retrieved July 2006 at: http://pegasus.cc.ucf.edu/~gallaghr/paris2000.html

Gallagher, S. (2005) *How the Body Shapes the Mind* (Oxford, Clarendon Press).

Greer, G. (1984) *Sex and Destiny: The politics of human fertility* (London, Secker and Warburg).

Grosz, E. (1995) *Space Time and Perversion: The politics of bodies* (New York, Routledge).

Heidegger, M. (1993/1978) *Basic Writings*, D. Farrell Krell, trans. (New York, Harper Collins Publishers).

Kalantzis, M. & Martin, B. (2006) *Border Knowledges, Global Learning: Global new learning*. Retrieved July 2006 at: http://www.borderknowledges.info/research/global%5Flearning.html

Kirby, V. (1997) *Telling Flesh: The substance of the corporeal* (New York & London, Routledge).

McPeck, J. E. (1981) *Critical Thinking and Education* (New York, St Martin's Press).

Merleau-Ponty, M. (1962/1945) *Phenomenology of Perception* (London, Routledge & Kegan Paul).

Merleau-Ponty, M. (1998/1964) The Visible and the Invisible, in: W. McNeill & K. S. Feldman (eds), *Continental Philosophy: An anthology* (Oxford, Blackwell Publishers), pp. 167–175.

O'Donovan-Anderson, M. (ed.) (1996) *The Incorporated Self: Interdisciplinary perspectives on embodiment* (Lanham, MD & London, Rowman & Littlefield Publishers).

Wilson, E. (2004a) Gut Feminism, *Differences: A Journal of Feminist Cultural Studies*, 15:3, pp. 66–94.

Wilson, E. (2004b) *Psychosomatic: Feminism and the neurological body* (Durham, NC & London, Drake University Press).

4

Schools as Places of Unselving: An educational pathology?

MICHAEL BONNETT

Introduction

There is a long tradition of seeing education as at least in part concerned with the development of the individual. For example, the enduring notion of liberal education initiated by Plato *inter alia* gives a central place to the good of the individual soul in its pursuit of knowledge and truth, the longstanding notion of Bildung orientates education around the idea of self-formation, and other influential overtly person-centred views of education such as child- and learner-centred clearly valorize the individual. Furthermore, in liberal democratic societies self-expression in the sense of freedom of individual thought and action is taken as a central value and it is a basic tenet of liberal democracy that within a framework of liberal moral values each individual is free to decide and pursue their own view of the good life and that education is in part a preparation for this. In addition, there is the view that the individual mind is—to put it no better at the moment—the place where knowledge, truth and understanding *occur* (as against the way that they may be *stored* in books, libraries, CD ROMS and websites, etc.). The basic point is that in the Western tradition education is centrally concerned with a range of ideas that are only intelligible in relation to some idea of a self. Understanding ideas of the self is thus central to understanding the idea of education in that tradition.

Having said this, there is no doubt in my mind that education should be a risky business: that in effect it must involve a degree of disturbance of the self. The task of the educator is not to indulge and hence to stultify the pupil, but to help them to change, to grow as persons. But, in my view, such self-transformation does not truly occur when ordered according to some grand plan articulated in sets of detailed objectives pre-specified independently of the teacher-learner interplay. The teacher must intend change without knowing in advance precisely what this change should or will be. Essentially, the teacher's task is to provide *occasions* for change by seeking opportunities to challenge pupils to take up the risk and respon-sibility of their own lives and to lend what support she may as pupils strive to do this.[1] To the extent that this occurs it will be in myriad ways and at many levels ranging from helping them to deepen or refine some specific aspect of their current engagement, to re-evaluating some core belief. Some element of disturbance of what is currently taken for granted (by both pupil and teacher) is never far away and, depending on how one defines it, nor is some threat to their personal identity. So change and disturbance are internal to education, but in my view these need to be conceived in organic rather than fragmented terms. It is with this is in mind that presently I will address the question of the school as a site for education.

First, one more introductory point. Inherent in all the above is the idea that it is difficult to make sense of many educationally significant notions without reference at some point to the idea of a conscious self, implying by this the notion of an entity that is separable in some significant sense from other selves and the rest of the cosmos in general. The idea of independence of some kind is implicit. However, the sense and degree to which this independence can be maintained has been problematized by many, including more recently those of a postmodernist turn of mind. (In an educational context, see, for example, Biesta, 2006; Stables, 2005.) Here, however, I wish to explore such issues as they are posed by certain elements of environmental concern, as I believe that these foreground some important considerations. It is a characteristic of many strands of environmental discourse that it either posits or assumes a notion of the self that is deeply relational, the very notion of ecology foregrounding ideas of interdependence. Indeed, in an essay that introduces a recent influential collection on environmental education research, it is claimed that the individual organism and its environment should be regarded as an integral system that constitute a single ecological unit, the 'fundamental particle' of ecology (Smyth, 2007). In a number of cases such an attitude has been framed in terms of an internal relationship between the idea of the individual and the idea of place. It is a strand of this line of thought that I wish to develop in what follows.

Unselving

> O if we but knew what we do
> When we delve or hew—
> Hack and rack the growing green!
> ... .
> After-comers cannot guess the beauty been.
> Ten or twelve, only ten or twelve
> Strokes of havoc unselve
> The sweet especial scene ...

These lines are taken from one of Gerard Manley Hopkins' better known poems called *Binsey Poplars*. It is a lament for the felling of a stand of trees that were intimately known to its author. I have been interested in different approaches to understanding the natural world and felt the question of what it would be for a natural thing to be 'unselved' fascinating. In a previous article on this topic (Bonnett, 2009) I expressed my response to these lines in the following way.

It seems to me that the notion of 'unselving' employed in the poem is seminal to giving an account of things in nature. Clearly Hopkins' poplars can be thought of as unselved in the obvious sense of being chopped down, but such 'physical' destruction is only one aspect of the unselving of a thing. The capacity of natural things to stand forth as the things that they are in their unique integrity does not consist primarily in some individual isolated objective existence. They are what they are for us in the context of an environment that they both constitute and are constituted by. But by 'environment' here I do not intend what ecologists and natural scientists often mean by the term: some sort of causal network or system in which organisms are nested and upon which they are bio-physically dependent. This is an abstraction, essentially an environment composed of functionaries. The key point is not that to extract living things from their natural environment will often result in physical harm both to themselves and others in the causal network— as, say, when a tree is removed to make way for a new road. It is rather that the tree, so displaced, has been withdrawn from the unique place—'especial scene'—that facilitates it in its occurring as the particular thing that it is. It has been withdrawn from, say, the play of sunlight on its limbs and leaves, from its movement in the breezes that stir at that spot, from the fall of its extending and diminishing shadow, from its posture in relation to its neighbours, from the sounds and sights of the birds that visit or inhabit it, from the dance of midges beneath its canopy as evening closes; that is to say from its unique and infinitely manifold contribution to the precise ambience of its neighbourhood. It upholds this neighbourhood—contributes to the unique and ever-changing qualities of its space—and is upheld by it. In other words it participates in a *place-making*, and is constituted as the thing that it is through this participation. Thus—to take one example—removed from its neighbours the posture of the tree might make little sense and we would have to 'read them in' to understand, say, both the precise shape and distribution of it foliage and the significance of this for the ambience of its neighbourhood.

This account foregrounds a number of overlapping features that I take to con-tribute to the individuality of a particular thing in nature: ideas of neighbourhood; inherence; relationality; dynamic, reciprocal participation; mutual sustaining. It also emphasizes that nothing that we encounter is unplaced—and reminded me that Heidegger speaks of place as the 'locale of the truth of Being'—by which I take him to mean that Being is unconcealed—i.e., things come to presence—not in some abstract uniform mathematical space-time framework, but in particular locally structured places. One never encounters such things as say a tree in blossom in uniform space, only neutered objects devoid of vigour and intrinsic significance. And overall, we have a way of looking at selfhood that moves away from a more atomistic position to one that is more (but certainly not exclusively) relational. The idea is not that there is not a perfectly good sense in which the re-located tree is the 'same' tree, but that there might be an important—perhaps more important— sense in which, also, it is not. It is not the same tree in the sense that its manner of being present is not the same. It shows up in experience very differently when re-located from its woodland 'home' to, say, a city square or shopping precinct. The particular self (i.e., selving) that is possible in the original 'especial place' has been destroyed. In more general terms, this offers an invitation to view the self not predominantly in terms of, say, space-time or bio-physical/causal continuity, but in terms of the qualities of its presencing. This de-reification could be important in the educational context because it demands an on-going attentiveness to the fluid being of individual things—for example, in the case of pupils, an attentiveness to how they are from situation to situation, rather than a reliance on how they have been defined (e.g., by test, report, or the talk).

Hence, it occurs to me that those features of individuality noted above might be germane to understanding the individuality—the selfhood—of a person as a 'thing' both 'in' nature and 'outside' it. And if this is so, it might be instructive to explore the way in which conventional educational institutions such as schools impact upon such constitutive qualities of individuality, here bearing in mind that a fundamental aspect of the strongly relational nature of the self foregrounded by the above account, is that of *bodily* inherence in a place—that is to say, in a *particular* place. Amongst others, Merleau-Ponty (1962), has developed the idea of the body as a site of perception, learning and knowledge, and it seems clear that its movements express myriad sensitivities and accommodations to a proximate environment in terms of which that body, its movement and its environment, are initially rendered intelligible and from which the sense of its own being—self—continuously springs, and in which it is continuously anchored. Hence, the effects of change of place upon this aspect of selfhood might be worth exploring in the context of education. In so far as conventional educational institutions typically for many extract the individual from a home environment and place them in another that in many significant respects differs from—and perhaps is in tension or contradiction with—this, it would not be difficult to imagine a line of argument to the effect that such disruption is threatening and unhelpful to the development of selfhood. To what extent, if at all, might unselving occur, and would this be a good or a bad thing? Is a certain degree of unselving a necessary part of the maturing of the self? Essentially, what is at stake here is the nature of our inherence in the world and the world's inherence in us. In order to address this issue we need to pose the following question: How is participation in 'place' and 'neighbourhood' to be understood in the case of a *conscious* embodied being?

For a conscious being place-making—the reciprocal participating in the constitution of a neighbourhood and being conditioned by that neighbourhood—occurs in the space of intelligibles, significances. Arguably such a space is not to be equated with—i.e., 'tied' to—the space of 'purely physical' geographical locations. Notwithstanding that such geographical locations can have certain personal or cultural significances, one can, as it were, to a significant—perhaps very high—degree take one's personal significances with one as one moves from one geographical location to another. For example, what I might come to identify as certain core beliefs need not change—can be carried forward—as I move from one place to another. (Although this will depend on the quality of the new place and the manner of my travel.) Hence one need not be so radically 'unselved' by such a move as was claimed for the tree. But if one is removed from the milieu of those things/people in which one customarily has one's being, enjoys relationships, does not a degree of unselving occur? To take an extreme case: suppose that someone is forcibly removed from the family, companions, computer, books, music, furniture, vistas and so forth that, as customarily experienced and located, (at least in part) constitute their home. They are no longer able to participate in its daily routines and associations, to enjoy, say—and taking one small aspect—the familiar and yet always surprising garden views across the seasons, the blossom and shade of its trees, the demands for weeding, its promptings as a historical site of personal events, aspirations and imaginings. Necessary as certain circumstances might seem to make it, a child or an older person's being extracted from the milieu that this exemplifies and taken into 'care' might not be without its cost in terms of sense of self.[2]

Conversely, it might be argued that finding oneself in a strange environment might heighten one's sense of self—one becomes more self-conscious in negotiating unfamiliar artefacts and expectations, one feels more sharply defined against the surrounding other that is now unfamiliar rather than familiar. For the moment I leave this as a possibility, for first I would like to explore further this notion of 'promptings' and to ask whether it might be significant in understanding the relationship between the individual and the environment.

There is an obvious sense in which different places/situations/'neighbourhoods' prompt—call for—different responses: whether we are in the presence of a friend or a stranger, are at a birth or a burial, encounter a valley or a mountain. This is true both in general cultural terms and at a personal level and on many occasions is taken to depend on what are referred to as 'associations' that the place or occasion might have. But this way of putting it is already misleading in some cases. Such talk of associations sets things up in a way that suggests that this place exists prior to them, had some independent existence to which the associations subsequently became attached. This can be the reverse of experience. For Jane, say, this *is* the place where her husband is buried; the stone and the grass and the faded flowers speak of it through and through. This place *claims* her in this way—and it becomes part constitutive of who she is. She *is* the person who is so-claimed and to be other would require an act of severance on her part. It is true that this is an extreme case and has been simplified, but it is illustrative of a general phenomenon. We are *always* claimed by places. With a possible exception to be discussed presently, we are never unplaced—though our sense of this is often highly tacit and the claims that are made upon us vary greatly in quality and strength.

But no action is possible in the absence of place, nor any thought, including that of sense of self. They all presuppose a milieu of prompts and claims.

Returning now to the example of the vulnerable person removed from their home: precisely what is it that is lost from the self through such extraction? Particular promptings and opportunities, certainly. But the self can 'carry forward' the understandings and sensitivities that they might have awoken. And there is memory. But memory, however vivid, is always at a remove. While it contributes to—indeed, is necessary to—being in a world, it is not immediate in the same sense, and is wont to pale. How one *is* is neither purely a function of memory, nor sensitivity as a capacity, nor constructive capacity, but must involve active reception.[3] One *is* in one's dealings with a world—partly familiar, partly unfamiliar—that is taken as 'not me', 'other', in at least a minimal sense. But it must be other in a *self-assuring* sense of being a place that is to some degree receptive to the self, actively accepts it, provides as it were the questions to its replies as well as the replies to its questions. That is to say a *mutual anticipation* (and invitation) of self and world is in play in which each is called forth.

On this account, self-assurance and intelligibility are inextricably interwoven. This acknowledges an affective aspect of being in a world that includes our bodily apprehension of where we are: the sense—i.e. feeling—that however hostile the situation, some aspects at least 'mesh' with one's anticipatory structure. Without this minimum level of felt continuity, the situation could not even be experienced as hostile because there is no foothold for understanding it. One is, as it were in freefall. This returns us to the possible exception mentioned above: the case where a place has no self-assuring features, that is, lacks any intelligibility whatsoever. Then we are truly adrift; literally, lost—one might say dissolved—in space. Put differently, such a radical state of affairs becomes unintelligible if we *are* understandingly. The notion (and experience) of being lost is derivative on the notion of place. With the complete confounding of anticipation follows the complete dissolution of both place and self. An unknown or mysterious place may breed anxiety, but the fully no-place breeds no-thing and no-self.

Anticipation

The chair anticipates sitting, the table food, the moon ... ? What does the moon anticipate? The upward stare? Yes: 'Look at the moon!'

While perhaps few today would argue for the pre-existing fully autonomous, disengaged, self of classical rationalism (and perhaps liberalism?) even as a theoretical construct, it remains a useful contrasting idea for differentiating more relational notions of the self. One such commonly experienced relational aspect is that of the importance of geographical and cultural origins to many people. While such an emphasis can bring dangers of a philosophy of 'blood and soil', ideas of a 'rootedness' in culture and/or place as constituents of self (identity) are frequently encountered. Environmental psychologists make the point that selfhood is seriously conditioned by sense of place and hence that human beings are fundamentally geographical beings. Not only, as some have it, can you not 'take the country out of the boy', if you take the boy out of the country, somehow his ability to *be* himself can be reduced. The necessary possibility of mutual anticipation of self and world is eroded. But might not the disruption of such anticipation be emancipatory through provoking new kinds of receptiveness, sensitivity? This raises the issue of what such anticipation invites. Perhaps if it were interpreted as highly routinized it would indeed seem to exclude or diminish the element of receptivity. And some uses of the term in everyday discourse suggest this as when, for example, a hotel recommends itself as anticipating the needs of its guests by providing a set of facilities and procedures that are on hand to support and reinforce a certain lifestyle. But the anticipation experienced on a fine spring morning by the walker as she sets off, or of the fisherman as he approaches the riverbank at dawn, or that of the trysting lover, is of a very different calibre. Here anticipation is experienced as an openness to and embracing of the unknown that is to come—the challenges and the sights, the smells, the textures, the ambiences and surprises of, say, different spots and times of day. It speaks of a keen attentiveness. Such anticipation quickens life, gives a heightened sense of being. It is a form of futurity, and of ecstasis.

Also, there is a sense in which everything we do involves anticipation: the gardener that the soil will yield to her spade, the sitter that the chair will bear his weight, the walker that the earth will bear her up, the reader that the text has a meaning. Often these are not conscious expectations, but are thoroughly implicit in the very movements/behaviour of the limbs of the gardener and walker, in the very act of scanning the text by the reader—indeed, in the act of opening the book or envelope. Anticipation pervades our being at many levels and it lies at the heart of the constant delicate, intelligent, adjustments that we make within our environment—the above examples intended to indicate that the intelligence involved here is often bodily.

What is the point here of speaking of mutual anticipations rather than simply speaking of significances? There is a sense in which the latter are achievements (however fluctuating or ephemeral), whereas the former are processes of directedness—understandings, yes, but *understandings in motion*. They are arisings of fit, occurrings of fittingness, aspects of the flow of intentionality. It might be thought that the notion of 'expectations' comes closer and, indeed, it is a frequently used term, but it denotes something perhaps that is still too abstract and explicitly statable, too cerebral. It seems to make more sense to say that the body anticipates, say, a fall rather than that it expects such. Figuratively, the dawn chorus anticipates rather than expects the new day.

Returning now to the liberating potential of removal from a familiar place: if this extraction is so radical as to stymie all anticipations it occludes a place for intelligibility to occur. And if too many anticipations are confounded or made redundant one's ability to inhere in a place—to be rooted—which is a central part of one's being in a world, is compromised: one is in danger of being pathologically unselved. This can become salient for educational institutions in a range of contexts.

Specific instances would include that of transition situations, or that of an ongoing 'mismatch' between a pupil and the school environment—whether this be in terms of individual proclivities or more general cultural formations such as those emanating from spiritual belief, bodily self-image, felt age, local environment (such as rural, urban, maritime, mountain, plains, etc), in addition to now rather worn notions of class, race, and gender. More generally, in so far as formal schooling is organized around a pre-specified curriculum, this necessarily tends to insulate learning from the free play of mutual anticipation. It therefore inclines teachers to an indifference to those ways of being in the world and of sense-making that spring from pupils' own emplaced experiences. This drains the intelligibility of the things that they encounter and learn of an important aspect of its vigour.

Furthermore, in educational institutions strongly influenced by Western rationality the focus of learning is on the universal. Hence it valorizes the abstract over the particular and the cerebral over the tactile, and, for example, third person over first person understandings of the body and of bodily experience. An overweening objectivation comes into play that reifies the flow of attunement produced by the free play of mutual anticipation and casts reference to the inherent fluidity and mystery of experience as obfuscation. The sense of what is not, what remains concealed, in what is—the sense of constant motion between what is present and what is withdrawn—is occluded. In such ways learning (and self-knowledge) become essentially fragmented and things in experience become products of calculation rather than exploratory sensing. This turn away from the value of the self's own emplaced experience is reflected in the general lack of space and time allowed to pupils for the enactment, evaluation and assimilation of what is taught so that it can find authentic expression in the pupil's on-going mode of being. Schools compound such pathologies when through their language and rituals they dress up self-denying ordinances (such as the disciplines associated with disengaged intellectual mastery, efficiency, and 'effective' analytic thinking) as self-affirming experiences. This overarching ethos is reinforced by standard assessment procedures that take little or no account of the significance of the intimately felt, nor such experientially important phenomena as gesture, intonation, humour (which can be a particularly perceptive kind of understanding and that is intimately bound up with situated anticipations), and continuity of learning with the self's own motives. Further to this, important questions are raised about the desirability and the undesirability of adapting to—embracing—'what at first wore a hideous mien' (Dewey, 1971, p. 28).

At this point I would like to sharpen up some of the issues by referring to some interesting discussion of what might be considered to be a counterbalancing, if not conflicting, idea: that of 'departures'.

Departures

Drawing on New England Transcendentalists—and particularly Stanley Cavell's commentary on their thinking—Paul Standish has developed an engaging perspective on the importance of this notion for self-development.[4] Here space permits only that I give some flavour of his position through the following sample of points.

Standish notes that whereas for Heidegger relation to a particular place that is the 'homeland' of our thought is necessary for proper dwelling and that the essential character of this is first revealed by the measure-taking of the poet (p. 115), for Emerson, the flow of poetic imagination is not to be understood in terms of home and settlement. Rather, it seeks new ways to actualize its energy, releasing and realizing new intensities of experience (p. 117). Approving this latter approach, Standish suggests that we 'should regard our lives as an opportunity at every point, with neither established foundation nor final settlement, but with every occasion an occasion for new departure' (pp. 129–130). Hence in his reading of Henry Thoreau's *Walden* Standish detects that:

> There is an increasing demand to take up the occasions of one's experience in such a way that one departs from one's settled and accustomed ways of understanding them, in order that one should seek possibilities of new departure—and *this not only at the level of one's larger decisions in life but also in one's daily engagement with language and life ...* (p. 132) [My emphases]

> In sum, it requires being ready to leave what you think is yours (your possessions, *you*), and so a readiness for departure, *where readiness is not*

something for which you consciously prepare but more like a receptiveness to the
new and a release from the hold of the past. And so, with Thoreau's
celebrated pun, morning (the orientation towards the future) is close
to mourning (loss, departure): mourning becomes morning. (p. 133) [My
emphases]

There is much here with which to agree if (as my emphases encourage) this is
interpreted as recommending an openness to new facets and depths of significance
in the familiar. But it should not be overlooked that this frequently requires a
patient attendance upon, and growing feel for, aspects of a place, and should not
necessarily invite a disparaging attitude towards habit, sense of belonging, and
responsibility in the longer term. This is not to deny that on occasion departures
in the bolder sense of quitting one place for another can be stimulating, but it does
question privileging this in any general way over the satisfactions and enrichment
to be obtained from settlement. (Perhaps a useful parallel can be drawn here with
developing a long term relationship with a person.) Kant and Heidegger, both of
whom travelled relatively little and enjoyed an enduring affection and respect for
one place for much of their lives, were amongst the most creative of philosophers.
There are those who claim never to tire of exploring and celebrating the same
place—or indeed, sometimes the same underlying thought. Some devote themselves
to their garden, local woodland, river, lake or region (as Thomas Hardy did to
'Wessex'), arguably without nett loss to the meaningfulness of their lives.

Standish goes on to recommend rejection of fixed identities that are the result
of custom or desire and observes that:

> ... contrary to popular readings of Thoreau, it is not this particular place
> [Walden Pond] that is the heart of the matter: what is more important is
> the possibility, or perhaps the principle, of this combination of particular
> attachments (the regimes of living attuned to them, the commitment
> appropriate to them) with a readiness for departure—before, as it were,
> they fossilize or perhaps came to be romanticized or to parody themselves.
> (p. 134)

Thus far it seems possible to give a reading of these ideas that is not only consistent
with the view that I have been developing, but that is positively sympathetic to it.
But in what follows something more radical and less acceptable appears, and that
seems to require that we revise such a reading and revisit our reservations concerning
the way that custom is portrayed. Standish invites us to consider favourably Herman
Hesse's assertion that when a circle of our life presents itself as 'home', we grow
weary: 'only she who is ready to journey forth/will escape habit's paralysis', and
Emerson's claim that, around every circle another circle can be drawn (p. 135).
These are taken to illustrate what Cavell speaks of as 'The essential immigrancy of
the human, a further formulation of the self's non-integrity' (p. 136).

Yet, how far is it defensible to align, even metaphorically, ideas of 'home' with
weariness, and 'habit' with paralysis? And in what sense, if any, is the privileging of
'immigrancy' and 'non-integrity' in characterizing the self appropriate? This whole

anti-conservative mindset is brought into question by thinkers such as Michael Oakeshott. In his essay 'The tower of Babel' (and elsewhere) he makes the point that 'habits of affection and behaviour' are key to a civilized way of living, that custom is not inert, unreceptive, and that it is a mistake to equate stability with rigidity:

> ... custom, we have been taught, is blind. It is, however, an insidious piece of misobservation: custom is not blind, it is only 'blind as a bat'. And anyone who has studied a tradition of customary behaviour (or a tradition of any sort) knows that both rigidity and instability are foreign to its character ... Indeed, no traditional way of behaviour, no traditional skill ever remains fixed; its history is one of continuous change. It is true that the change that it admits is neither great nor sudden; but then, revolutionary change is usually the product of the eventual overthrow of an aversion from change, and is characteristic of something that has few internal resources of change. And the appearance of changelessness in a morality of traditional behaviour is an illusion that springs from the erroneous belief that the only significant change is either that which is induced by selfconscious activity or is, at least, observed on the occasion. The sort of change that belongs to this form of moral life is analogous to the change to which a living language is subject: nothing is more habitual or customary than our ways of speech, and nothing is more continuously invaded by change ... habits of moral conduct show no revolutionary changes because they are never at rest. (Oakeshott, 1991, p. 471)

Here the metaphor of the 'blindness' of the bat brings out the fine tuned non-cerebral sensing that informs the ever-occurring change that is rooted in and responsive to the subtle nuances of its environment. The point is made that language—that great vehicle of thought and receptivity—is grounded in habit and custom: would disintegrate without them, and that the (revolutionary) need to move on—'depart'—can be seen to reflect a situation where the ability to be sustained by internal resources has been lost through the lack or demise of sensitivity to the infinite possibilities and ever-changing countenances of, for example a natural place or certain forms of occupation—where, indeed, the person has lost or deserted its (and maybe their own) genius. Here, an ultimately enervating cosmopolitanism has become ascendant and breadth has subverted depth. And the overweening ambition of a tower of Babel of self-gratification breeds confusion and results in an immigrancy that is a corrosive dispersion of meanings and behaviours. Integrity of self, of tradition and of place are finely interwoven and it might be thought that their loss is no small price to pay in the (deluded) pursuit of some essentially free-floating existence.

Let me make it clear here that I am not attempting to mount an argument that forbids the seeking of a 'change of scene', 'fresh pastures', nor one that denies the value of being open to the new in the old and the fresh in the familiar. And certainly in many contexts there can be good reason for seeking to disrupt settled ways of seeing and categorizing perhaps for the power relationships that they express, their wrong headedness, or, indeed, because they have become stultifying. In principle I have no quarrel with such arguments. What seems less defensible is any general assumption of the superiority of a life that valorizes change and departure in the strong sense, that seeks to be on the move, sojourning rather than rooted, universal rather than autochthonous; a life that is 'experienced' rather than dwelt. Some might chose to live thus, but for many such a life is neither a possible choice nor a desideratum and it is far from clear why it should be preferred to say—and to give an extreme counterpoint—a life more expressive of the conservationist outlook of an indigenous culture that some strands of environmental concern attempt to retrieve and reinstate. Attachment to and feeling of responsibility to a particular place, and patient initiation into the bodily intimate, slowly accumulated, intergenerational knowledge of it are not available to the passer through, and yet for some constitute a deeply satisfying way of life. And for others part, at least, of the appeal of travel is the prospect of the return home. A central issue can be not the achievements of the endless journey, but the draw of the welcoming home—the quality of the engagements that it affords. To be 'at home' anywhere and every-where is to be both homeless and self-less.

Conclusion: Schools as Places of Unselving

The title of this chapter asks whether as places of unselving, there might be aspects of schools that are pathological in educational terms. This is framed as a question because it seems to me that the issue is not straightforward. It seems clear that at certain times and in varying degree schools as institutions are places of unselving in the terms in which I have elaborated that idea. For example, at 'transition points' the reciprocal anticipation of student and place can be disturbed at many levels: from relations with the people to relations with the furniture and implements of work; from the ambiences in which different places in the new school invite participation to the aspects of posture and clothing that are both explicitly and implicitly sanctioned. Singly and combined these can contribute salient sets of prompts and claims that can confound those former anticipations that constitute the life-world of the entering pupil. Perhaps she is encouraged to write with her right rather than her left hand, the furniture shapes her body in an unaccustomed—perhaps for her, uncomfortable—way, her neighbour is someone she did not—and perhaps would not—choose, her emotional gestures elicit puzzling and sometimes hostile responses, her humour is rebuffed, and so forth. In such ways she might feel 'out of place'. This, all in a superordinate situation that she did not choose and to which she is required to subscribe, indeed towards which she senses that she is required to show enthusiasm and commitment. Of course accommodation (of a kind) is often, but not always, possible. 'See how quickly she has settled in!' ... 'has found her place' ... (that is, now 'knows her place'). Such a happy outcome! Euphemisms for subjection and subjectivation abound.

   It might be objected here that moving from one home, institution, workplace, region, to another is a common and often desirable feature of life in general. My point, of course, is not that all such cases of transition involve pathological unselving, but that the danger is there and that it can be acute in some cases—as for example with a timid child when the imperatives under which the school operates strongly conflict with those of the home. The key underlying question is what kinds and degree of self-assurance are being offered and what kinds and degree of self-disconcertion? And when are they edifying and when pathological? Clearly, it would be inappropriate to generalize on the particularities of such matters; this paper can only attempt to draw attention to the issues and some of the structural features that are in play.

When, then, is significant disturbance of anticipation a source of maturation and when a dislocation that leads to a diminution of the potential for selfhood and creative self-assertion? *Of course* one needs to learn to adapt to—and in some circumstances utilize—what one might term different registers of being, and to negotiate new and perhaps disconcerting places. On the view offered in this chapter the educational need is for opportunities for experimental play that enables the self to situate and re-situate itself; to provide challenges that can be experienced as resonating with the field of anticipations of the learner. And since only the learner can know whether this resonance occurs, essentially the challenges must have the quality of invitations rather than impositions. The same consideration applies to the issue of what counts as a challenge—and what is experienced as disruption rather than (potentially constructive) disturbance. Attention needs to be paid to a student's feelings of comfort and discomfort, which might often be a response to the ambience of the place of learning (including the way in which significant others make their presence felt), rather than the cognitive substance of learning. What is experienced as an overwhelming and destructive challenge in one such peopled place, might be greeted with keen anticipation in another. This puts the quality of the teacher-pupil relationship at the heart of education.

Today, current levels of passivity, disaffection and truancy suggest that renewed attention needs to be given to the ways in which students do and do not inhere in the places in which they are compelled to undertake their formal education. What millieu of anticipations does a school offer? How deep, extensive and engaging are the prompts and the calls that are both self-assuring and challenging? What freedoms and encouragements are pupils given in responding to them? Part of the issue here can be the extent to which there is positive nurturing of inherence in their own place: particular, local and regional, as well as universal and global. Another part can be the inherent mis-separation of cerebral and bodily satisfaction and the asymmetry of the relative importance placed on each. A focus on place draws attention to dimensions of engagement, sensitivity and response that by far outstrip what formal education normally takes as central. Levels of pathological unselving can occur as a result of the often impoverished—if not downright antagonistic—environment provided for the sensuous, physically initiating and active embodied individual. Fuller acknowledgement of this than is often currently the case would be a first step towards addressing a significant educational pathology.

Acknowledgement

I wish to thank Gloria Dall'Alba for her very helpful comments on an earlier version of this chapter.

Notes

1. I have argued for this in Bonnett (1994) Part Three.
2. This is not to deny that there can be circumstances in which the home itself can become a place of pathological unselving.
3. In introducing the term 'reception', I want to question the current emphasis on the learner as active agent that occludes or derides an essential personal passivity involved in authentic perception and therefore learning—an openness and responsibility to things themselves, to letting them 'shine through', for example, our overweening web—sometimes veil—of instrumental purposes. As, for example, when the individuality of the pupil is subverted to externally devised 'educational'/economic targets and standards, or when the same attitude is adopted towards the natural world.
4. In Smeyers, P., Smith, R., Standish, P. (2007) *The Therapy of Education*, Ch. 8.

References

Biesta, G. (2006) *Beyond Human Learning. Democratic Education for a Human Future* (Boulder, Colorado, Paradigm Publishers).

Bonnett, M. (1994) *Children's Thinking* (London, Cassell).

Bonnett, M. (2009) Education, sustainability and the metaphysics of nature, in: M. McKenzie, H. Bai, B. Jickling (eds), *Fields of Green. Re-storying Education* (Cresshill, US, Hampton Press).

Dewey, J. (1971) *The Child and the Curriculum* (Chicago, University of Chicago Press).

Manley-Hopkins, G. (1979) *Gerard Manley Hopkins The Major Poems* (London, J. M. Dent).

Merleau-Ponty, M. (1962) *The Phenomenology of Perception* (London, Routledge & Kegan Paul).

Oakeshott, M. (1991) The tower of Babel in *Rationalism in Politics and Other Essays*, New expanded edition (Indianapolis, Liberty Fund).

Smyth, J. (2007) Environment and education: a view of a changing scene, in: A. Reid and W. Scott (eds), *Researching Education and the Environment: Retrospect and Prospect* (London, Routledge).

Smeyers, P., Smith, R., Standish, P. (2007) *The Therapy of Education* (Basingstoke, Palgrave Macmillan).

Stables, A. (2005) *Living and Learning as Semiotic Engagement. A New Theory of Education* (New York, Edwin Mellen Press).

5

Learning Professional Ways of Being: Ambiguities of becoming

Gloria Dall'Alba

Entry to the professions requires a transition period in which aspiring professionals are prepared for the challenges of practice in their chosen profession. Professional education programs offered by higher education institutions are often charged with this task of preparation for professional practice. These programs typically focus on developing specific knowledge and skills to be applied in practice contexts within and beyond the educational program. How can a nurse graduate without knowing about treatment of wounds, it might be argued; or an architect without knowing how to locate a building on a designated site? Those professions that require registration in order to practise tend to direct focus still more strongly to knowledge and skills that must be acquired during professional education.

While knowledge and skills are necessary, they are insufficient for skilful practice and for transformation of the self that is integral to achieving such practice. When we concentrate our attention on epistemology—or what students know and can do—we fail to facilitate and support such transformation. A focus on epistemology occurs at the expense of ontological considerations relating to who students are becoming. We expect professional education programs to lead to transformations associated with this process of becoming, for example, from student to engineer, historian, or medical practitioner. However, these transformations and, more specifically, processes of becoming, often go unacknowledged in theorising and practice relating to higher education programs. More recently, theorising about such programs has begun to take into account this ontological dimension (e.g. Barnett, 1997, 2004, 2005; Thomson, 2001; Dall'Alba, 2004, 2009; Barnacle, 2005; Dall'Alba & Barnacle, 2005, 2007). The purpose of professional education programs can then be conceptualised in terms of developing ways of being the professionals in question, rather than simply as a source of knowledge and skills acquisition.

In extending previous research, this chapter explores what it means to develop 'professional ways of being' (Dall'Alba, 2004), where the focus is becoming the professionals in question, not simply knowing as an end in itself. The chapter begins by foregrounding ontological dimensions of education, drawing upon ideas from Martin Heidegger. Maurice Merleau-Ponty's notion of ambiguity in our relation to the world is then used as a way of elaborating what ontological education means for learning professional ways of being. Against the background of these analyses, professional education is reconfigured as a process of becoming.

Education as Transforming Ways of Being

Re-thinking ontology, including the being of human and non-human beings, is a recurring theme in Heidegger's magnum opus, *Being and Time*, as well as in many of his later works. Heidegger considered it necessary to clarify what it means to be human if we are more fully to comprehend thinking and knowing as modes of being human. He regarded modes of knowing, such as architecture, biology, history and so on, as ways of being human (1962/1927, p. 408, § 357; see also pp. 88–90 § 61–62). This means that if we are fully to understand knowing within various forms of professional practice, we must understand the being of those who know.

Central to Heidegger's ontology is his concept of 'being-in-the-world', which emphasises that we are always already embedded in, and entwined with, our world, not simply contained within it. As Heidegger points out, we typically are absorbed in a range of activities and projects with others that involve the use of tools or equipment and production of artefacts. We generally carry out these activities and projects in a mode of 'average everydayness'. That is, we are usually absorbed in, and take for granted, the routine and everyday, so we generally do not place them under scrutiny. Operating in a mode of average everydayness enables us to complete our tasks and activities.

As we go about our activities and projects, we take up possibilities that are open to us. For example, we may seek out opportunities to interact with particular people or take action that sets us on a new career path. For Heidegger, being human means having possibilities, or possible ways to be (1962/1927, p. 40, § 42). We also understand ourselves in terms of possibilities (p. 185, § 145). This directedness to possibilities means we are continually in a process of becoming; more specifically, we are already (oriented to) what we are 'not yet' (pp. 185–186, § 145). For example, if we make a commitment to become a teacher, musician, or economist, what we seek to know, how we act, and who we are is directed by and to this commitment, which organises and constitutes our becoming.

In describing this process of becoming, Iain Thomson points to a distinction made by Heidegger (1962/1927, pp. 185–186 § 145) between 'being-possible' and 'ability-to-be':

> As Blattner nicely puts it, 'there are two functions here: opening up the range of possibilities, and pressing ahead into one of them'. We become what we are 'not yet', then, by pressing ahead into (or projecting ourselves upon) our projects. (Thomson, 2004, p. 450)

Through taking up some possibilities and not others, we contribute to forming our present and future, with the anticipation and anxiety that this entails. Given that we are entwined with our world, the possibilities open to us are not limitless, as discussed below.

Not only do human beings have a range of possible ways to be, but also our being is an issue for us; it matters to us who we are and who we are becoming. We are 'a being who takes a stand on its being and is defined by that stand' (Thomson, 2004, p. 453). The stands we take have particular significance in that:

... the very way reality shows up for us is filtered through and circumscribed by the stands we take on ourselves, the embodied life-projects which organize our practical activities and so shape the intelligibility of our worlds. (p. 444)

In potentially forming and shaping the stands we take, education can have a key part to play in who we are becoming: in what we come to know, how we act, and who we are.

Heidegger highlights and offers insights into ontological dimensions of education in the context of his broader project of re-thinking ontology. He argues for an ontological turn as a way forward for higher education (Thomson, 2001; Dall'Alba & Barnacle, 2005, 2007). Indeed, Thomson argues that re-thinking education on ontological grounds is an enduring theme for Heidegger, although he points out it is largely unacknowledged in the research literature about Heidegger's work. Thomson notes that 'a radical re-thinking of education—in a word, an ontologization of education—forms one of the deep thematic undercurrents of Heidegger's work, early as well as late' (2004, p. 439). For Thomson, these ideas permeate *Being and Time* with a 'quiet presence' likely to be noted only by those already familiar with Heidegger's philosophy of education (p. 440). Michael Bonnett (2002), too, argues that Heidegger puts forward powerful ideas for education in both his early and later work. Bonnett illustrates, for example, how Heideggerian notions of teaching and learning call into question an instrumental view of education that has relevance for our times. (See also Dall'Alba, 2005; Dall'Alba & Barnacle, 2005, 2007 for similar arguments in relation to higher education.)

A central purpose of education, according to Heidegger, is transformation of the self. Drawing on Plato, he calls into question education that is concerned with 'merely pouring knowledge into the unprepared soul as if it were some container held out empty and waiting. On the contrary real education lays hold of the soul itself and transforms it in its entirety' (Heidegger, 1998/1967, p. 167).[1] This transformation of the self can be achieved by interrogating what we take for granted about our world and ourselves; by challenging assumptions we make about them and have historically made. In other words, again drawing on Plato, transformation of the self involves 'turning around the whole human being. It means removing human beings from the region where they first encounter things and transferring and accustoming them to another realm where beings appear' (1998/1967, p. 167).[2] According to Thomson, the purpose is 'to bring us full circle back to ourselves, first by turning us away from the world in which we are most immediately immersed, then by turning us back to this world in a more reflexive way' (2001, p. 254). When the familiar or everyday appears in a new light, the way is open for other possibilities, other ways of being. Becoming a teacher, physiotherapist or lawyer, then, involves 'turning around' or transforming the self. Through interrogating and re-shaping assumptions about what it means to teach, provide physiotherapy or apply the rule of law, new ways of being are opened to aspiring professionals and can begin to take shape. It is not only a question of epistemology but, more particularly, of ontology.

When aspiring professionals seek to enter a profession, the practices they learn to embody have their own routines, histories and traditions. Learning to engage with these to the extent they are manifest in the present and relevant for the future is a necessary part of learning professional ways of being. Transformation of the self in becoming a professional is, then, not a wholly individual or isolated enterprise. As Heidegger points out, in our everyday practices we are entwined with our world and we interpret ourselves in terms of the reflected light of that world, but we are also entwined in traditions that tend to cover over what is being passed on down the generations (1962/1927, pp. 42–43 § 21). In other words, the traditions of which we are a part tend to be taken for granted and are not transparent to us: the fish is the last to discover water. Becoming a professional, then, involves transformation of the self through embodying the routines and traditions of the profession in question, although this is not straightforward, as discussed below.

Our Ambiguous Relation to Our World[3]

While Heidegger situates his arguments about the need to ontologise higher education within the context of our entwinement with our world, Merleau-Ponty points to the body as the medium for this embeddedness in, and engagement with, our world:

> The body is the vehicle of being in the world, and having a body is, for a living creature, to be intervolved in a definite environment, to identify oneself with certain projects and be continually committed to them ... . I am conscious of my body *via* the world ... [and] I am conscious of the world through the medium of my body. (1962/1945, p. 82)

Here Merleau-Ponty refers not merely to the physical body as a set of interconnected organs, but the body *as lived*. This 'lived body' is a site and source of ambiguity:

> When I press my two hands together, it is not a matter of two sensations felt together as one perceives two objects placed side by side, but of an ambiguous set-up in which both hands can alternate the roles of 'touching' and 'being touched'. (p. 93)

Expressed differently, 'I apprehend my body as a subject-object, as capable of "seeing" and "suffering"' (p. 95).

Merleau-Ponty provides insight into our ambiguous relation to our world when he argues that 'ambiguity is of the essence of human existence, and everything we live or think has always several meanings' (p. 169). This ambiguity opens up possible ways to know, to act and to be that interrelate with the stands we take on our being. For example, a teacher may feel irritation at the lack of engagement of 'problem' students and/or wonder about the relation between their lack of engagement and the teaching they experience. Such ambiguity provides openings for re-thinking our taken-for-granted assumptions, for example, about what it means to teach and to be a committed teacher. In highlighting ambiguity in our relation to our world,

Merleau-Ponty resists a common tendency to isolate and categorise, instead demonstrating that our categories and entities spill over into one another. Exploring implications of this ambiguous relation to our world for professional education can enable us to better grasp what it means to learn professional ways of being.

Ambiguity of Becoming

Several features of learning to become professionals are outlined in this section as we explore the ambiguity that is integral to our professional lifeworld. These features are principally explored in relation to the period of transition from aspiring to practising professionals, although they also have relevance for continuing to learn as professionals. The features include: *continuity* over time *with change* in ways of being professionals; *possibilities* in the ways we can be *with constraints* on those possibilities; *openness* in taking up possibilities *with resistance* to doing so; and *individuals* who are becoming professionals *with others* involved in that process. Attending to, and dwelling with, these ambiguities—while recognising them as ambiguities, not simply conflicts to be resolved—can open possibilities for enriching professional education programs and making these programs more meaningful for those who are learning ways of being that relate to particular professions.

Continuity with Change

Both continuity and change occur through the passage of time as part of our everyday life. Our world today is both the world it was yesterday and a changed world. In some sense, we are the persons we were yesterday and will be tomorrow, but also not the same. For Heidegger and Merleau-Ponty, temporality—or historicity— is not only inevitable but also central to being human. Both these scholars resist the everyday conception that we are contained in time as it flows around us, perhaps carrying us along: 'I am not in space and time, nor do I conceive space and time; I belong to them, my body combines with them and includes them' (Merleau-Ponty, 1962/1945, p. 140).

   According to Heidegger, we are our past. The past not only 'pushes along "behind" ', but is also our way of being in the present, which anticipates and creates the future (1962/1927, p. 17 § 20). The past does not determine the present or future, but it opens possible ways of being. The past, present and future do not form a linear trajectory, then, but the past opens a range of possibilities that can be taken up in the present, while directing us away from other possibilities. At the same time, the past becomes a resource in the present and for the future. Elizabeth Grosz considers temporality in a way that is reminiscent of Heidegger when she points out the past is never fixed nor determines the present and future, but inheres in them:

> Life is a becoming beyond what it is because the past, not fixed in itself, never fixes or determines the present and future but underlies them, inheres in them, makes them rich in resources, and forces them to differ from themselves. (Grosz, 2004, p. 255)

This folding of past into present, into future ensures continuity with change in our lives, while opening up a range of possible development trajectories. Even aspiring professionals who may have no prior experience of being an archaeologist, journalist or dentist bring with them some notion of what these professions entail that, initially at least, underpins their becoming. However, when these aspiring professionals gain entry to their chosen profession, they have undergone substantial change, not least in their ways of being professionals. This process of change with continuity continues throughout our professional lives; it is integral to both being professionals and continuing to learn as professionals (Webster-Wright, 2006), as well as integral to being human and continuing to learn, more generally. There is ambiguity, then, in who we are (becoming) as professionals through this enfolding of continuity with change.

For instance, aspiring teachers embarking on their studies in teacher education continue to be the persons they are in some respects, within the context of a world that continues to operate largely as before. At the same time, these teacher trainees undergo change in their capacity to teach and in their understanding of what teaching involves. As they learn to become teachers, both epistemology and ontology are involved. The teacher trainees continue to be who they are and to be recognisable to those who know them, while also being transformed.

Grosz, who draws upon Merleau-Ponty's concept of the lived body in some of her work (e.g. Grosz, 1994), describes this temporal ambiguity as doubling; allowing past, present and future to form a continuity:

> The present not only acts, it also consolidates, the past; it doubles itself as both present and past, actual and virtual. And it is only this doubling that enables it to resonate with the resources, the virtual, that the past endows to it and to the future (Grosz, 2004, p. 251).

Inherent in this continuity are the conditions for change in the future:

> The present acts, is active, makes. But what it makes is never self-identical, stable, given as such to the next moment. What it acts or makes is the condition of the transformative effects of the future. (p. 251)

For example, as trainee teachers learn to teach, their positive and negative experiences of being students in classrooms over several years can serve as a resource for their teaching. Threads carried forward from the past can serve as resources in the present, as well as providing openings for change that continues into the future. They may afford opportunities for interrogating and transforming understanding of teaching when teaching does not lead to the desired outcomes or students do not respond as expected. Temporality ensures, then, some degree of sameness or continuity, while opening up for other ways of being: 'inherence of the past in the present, for the capacity to become other' (Grosz, 2004, p. 252).

Possibilities with Constraints

The interweaving of continuity with change ensures some routines and regularities—including those permeated by domination or, conversely, by mutual respect—while at the same time there are openings for other possibilities; things could be otherwise. These possibilities are not limitless, however. Our possible ways of acting and of being are constrained by the specific situations we inhabit with their history and traditions. Familiar routines and ready-made solutions cover over the range of possibilities open to us in any situation as we go about our activities in a mode of average everydayness, which tends to be the path of least resistance. Our own past that we carry forward also places limits on the possibilities open to us. Heidegger points out that we 'grow into' a familiar way of interpreting ourselves that is reflected from our world. He argues that we understand ourselves in terms of this interpretation, which opens possibilities for being as well as constraining those possibilities (1962/1927, pp. 17–18 § 20).

For example, some teacher trainees may strive to engage their students in learning that is challenging and transformative. The efforts they make to achieve this are afforded opportunities, as well as constrained, by their understanding of themselves as teachers in interrelation with traditions of practice relating to teaching. Certain practices, such as involving students in assessing the work of their peers, may be considered acceptable by students and colleagues, while other practices, such as allowing students to determine their own course of study, may be regarded as inappropriate or negligent by some, while exciting or innovative by others. So, traditions of practice for teaching simultaneously open possibilities and constrain. These traditions interrelate with other changes in society, so that teacher trainees and/or experienced teachers may begin to challenge and transform the notion of what it means to teach through their practice.

Opening of possibilities and associated constraints also play out through the aspirations of those who seek to become professionals, although these aspirations may change over time. Doret de Ruyter and Jim Conroy (2002) point to the importance of 'ideal identity', or aspirations about what the person in question wants to be, for formation of a sense of self. They argue that these aspirations contribute to the formation of a sense of self 'as a result of: (a) clarifying what kind of person the individual wishes to be; and (b) an interrogation of how she sets about achieving her ideal identity, intimating what kind of person she is at a particular moment by virtue of the way in which she strives to achieve her ideal' (p. 509). Studies of workplace learning (e.g. Webster-Wright, 2006) demonstrate that failure to achieve an unrealistic ideal (perpetuated by organisations, professional associations and/or professionals themselves) can result in feelings of impostership; of never being good enough or as accomplished as others.

The ambiguity associated with possibilities and constraints does not operate in a neutral manner. Practice traditions and social structures constrain opportunities for some, while opening them to others. For instance, in Australian schools until around the 1960s (with exact dates varying from one part of the country to another) female teachers were forced to resign from permanent positions if they married, making teaching positions and promotions available to male teachers and female teachers who had never married. Bronwyn Davies (2003, 2005) describes constraints on contemporary university teachers arising from a neoliberal agenda, which she argues curtails creative or intellectual work. In short, power relations permeate professional practice and efforts to become professionals.

Openness with Resistance

In a context where power relations play out in concert with self-interpretation, we demonstrate openness to possibilities and opportunities that are presented to us, as well as resistance. Drawing upon Heidegger's work, Glenn Gray points out 'there is always a struggle to advance a new way of seeing things because customary ways and preconceptions about it stand in the way' (1968, p. xxi). At the same time, we demonstrate openness to possibilities in relation to, and sometimes by means of, these customary ways and preconceptions. This 'struggle' or interplay between openness and resistance can apply to any aspect of our relation to our world; it relates to individuals and professions as a whole.

While aspiring professionals often demonstrate some openness to learning new ways of knowing and acting, sustaining such changes so that they become incorporated into customary ways of being can be challenging. Interplay between openness and resistance not only challenges our knowing or actions, but also who we are and understand ourselves to be. For instance, innovative ideas brought by trainee teachers sometimes challenge pre-conceptions about teaching among experienced teachers, or vice versa. Challenges of this kind can occur for individuals, as well as flowing over to the profession as a whole. Addressing or resolving such tensions involves questioning assumptions, not only about what teaching involves, but also about what it means to be a teacher. Once again, not only epistemology but also ontology is at stake.

Interplay of openness with resistance is linked to the ways in which continuity in routines is interrupted or displaced by efforts toward renewal. Established routines and associated professional ways of being may exert themselves to such an extent that renewal of practice is obstructed. This can present difficulties for aspiring and recently graduated professionals, as well as for experienced professionals, who see the potential for improved practices but experience resistance or disapproval from others. Power differentials often play a key role in influencing the outcome of challenges to established routines and practices. However, where there is some openness to re-thinking assumptions and mutual respect among practitioners, new ways of acting and of being can come into play, bringing about a renewal of practice at both individual and collective levels.

Individuals with Others

It is evident from each of the preceding features of learning to become professionals that engaging with others is integral to the professional lifeworld, with language playing a key role. For Heidegger (1962/1927), being-in-the-world, more generally, necessarily incorporates being with others, including those who are only implicated, such as members of our profession who developed a tool we use but whom we may never meet. Heidegger also points out that through being with others, we learn to think and act as (the generalised) 'they' do. In learning to think and act as 'they' do, we also take a stand on those thoughts and actions, as well as on who we are becoming, even if this means we simply fall into line with how 'one' should think, act and be. For instance, aspiring teachers learn various ways in which one acts as a member of the teaching profession, while taking a stand on the ways and extent to which they will follow what one is expected to do. At the same time, being with others—including those within and outside the profession—extends possibilities for being, potentially enriching the process of becoming. Trainee teachers, for example, are likely to learn from their encounters with students and parents, as well as from colleagues.

The process of becoming a professional occurs, then, through continual interaction with other professionals, as well as those outside the professions. It is misleading to attempt to separate the individual from engagement with others in this process of becoming. Quite simply, an individual does not become a professional in isolation; conversely, a profession cannot exist without individual professionals. The two are interdependent and spill over into one another, as well as being entangled in the broader social world.

Reconfiguring Professional Education as a Process of Becoming

When we take seriously the ontological dimension of professional education and the ambiguities of learning to become professionals, professional education can no longer stop short after developing knowledge and skills. Acquisition of knowledge and skills is insufficient for embodying and enacting skilful professional practice, including for the process of becoming that learning such practice entails. Instead, when we take account of ontology, professional education is reconfigured as a process of becoming; an unfolding and transformation of the self over time. Contrary to what prevalent models of professional development would have us believe, this process is unlikely to occur in a predetermined or linear sequence (e.g. as proposed by Benner, 1984; Dreyfus & Dreyfus, 1986) but, rather, to follow a range of possible development trajectories (see Dall'Alba & Sandberg, 2006; Dall'Alba, 2009). This unfolding is open-ended and always incomplete.

Learning to become professionals entails integrating what aspiring professionals know and can do with who they are (becoming), including the challenges, risk, commitment and resistance that are involved. In other words, learning professional ways of being occurs through integration of knowing, acting and being the professionals in question (Dall'Alba, 2009; see also Dall'Alba, 2005; Dall'Alba & Barnacle, 2007). This means, for example, that teacher education programs cannot simply impart knowledge and skills to aspiring teachers. Instead, relevant knowledge and skills are embodied and enacted by those in these programs to varying extents and in a range of ways, in line with the social practice of teaching (see Dall'Alba, 2005, for further elaboration in relation to university teaching). For instance, teacher trainees learn to design learning activities and to assess what students have learned. As they do so, they develop their ways of knowing and acting in relation to designing learning and assessment, while at the same time extending and elaborating their understanding and embodiment of what it means to be a teacher. Referring to Heidegger's work, Thomson outlines the way in which our knowing, acting, and being are interrelated:

> Our very 'being-in-the-world' is shaped by the knowledge we pursue, uncover, and embody. [There is] a troubling sense in which it seems that we cannot help practicing what we know, since we are 'always already' implicitly shaped by our guiding metaphysical presuppositions. (2001, p. 250)

Conceptualising professional education programs in terms of an integration of knowing, acting and being further clarifies the inadequacy of a focus on epistemology (or knowing) in which ontology (or being and becoming) is overlooked. Efforts to treat knowing, acting and being as separate entities (e.g. through an emphasis on epistemology at the expense of ontology) fall short of what professional education programs can, and are expected to, achieve (see also Barnett, 1997, 2004, 2005; Heidegger, 1998/1967). Where this shortfall occurs, the most challenging task of learning professional ways of being through integration of these various aspects is left to the students themselves. At the same time, the part that professional education programs can and do play in forming and shaping professionals raises complex ontological and ethical questions. For instance, in what ways and to what extent is it appropriate to shape another's becoming? Whose knowing, acting and being serve as 'golden standards'? Questions such as these underpin the design and implementation of professional education programs, whether or not they are explicitly addressed in those programs.

Conclusion

In professional education programs, emphasising ontology means placing the focus on learning professional ways of being, that is, on becoming the professionals in question. In other words, it places emphasis on enabling students to integrate their ways of knowing, acting and being professionals. This conceptualisation has the potential to provide clearer direction for our efforts in designing professional education programs, as well as in challenging and supporting students who proceed through these programs.

Acknowledgements

A previous version of this chapter was presented as part of a symposium entitled Phenomenology in Education at the European Conference on Educational Research in Geneva in September, 2006. I am grateful to Michael Bonnett, John Bowden, Jörgen Sandberg, Moira von Wright and Melanie Walker whose careful reading and comments on an earlier version allowed me to improve this chapter. A University of Queensland research grant contributed to work done in completing the chapter.

Notes

1. As Heidegger points to the fallacy of a Cartesian separation of body and soul (or mind) (e.g. 1962/1927, p. 72, § 46), the term, soul, here is not to be understood in this sense, but in the sense outlined below.

2. Heidegger is using Plato's allegory of the cave to explore the relation between education and 'truth' or unhiddenness.
3. Discussing our relation to the world may give the impression we are independent of, and separable from, the world. Such a conceptualisation is at odds with the notion of an inevitable entwinement with our world, as discussed below, although contemporary language presents obstacles in developing ideas of this kind.

References

Barnacle, R. (2005) Research Education Ontologies: Exploring doctoral becoming, *Higher Education Research and Development*, 24, pp. 179–188.

Barnett, R. (1997) *Higher Education: A critical business* (Buckingham, SRHE & Open University Press).

Barnett, R. (2004) Learning for an Unknown Future, *Higher Education Research and Development*, 23, pp. 247–260.

Barnett, R. (2005) Recapturing the Universal in the University, *Educational Philosophy and Theory*, 37, pp. 785–797.

Benner, P. (1984) *From Novice to Expert: Excellence and power in clinical nursing practice* (San Francisco, Addison-Wesley).

Bonnett, M. (2002) Education as a Form of the Poetic: A Heideggerian approach to learning and the teacher-pupil relationship, in: M. A. Peters (ed.), *Heidegger, Education and Modernity* (Lanham, MD, Rowman & Littlefield), pp. 229–243.

Dall'Alba, G. (2004) Understanding Professional Practice: Investigations before and after an educational programme, *Studies in Higher Education*, 29, pp. 679–692.

Dall'Alba, G. (2005) Improving Teaching: Enhancing ways of being university teachers, *Higher Education Research and Development*, 24, pp. 361–372.

Dall'Alba, G. (2009) *Learning to be Professionals* (Dordrecht, The Netherlands, Springer).

Dall'Alba, G. & Barnacle, R. (2005) Embodied Knowing in Online Environments, *Educational Philosophy and Theory*, 37, pp. 719–744.

Dall'Alba, G. & Barnacle, R. (2007) An Ontological Turn for Higher Education, *Studies in Higher Education*, pp. 679–691.

Dall'Alba, G. & Sandberg, J. (2006) Unveiling Professional Development: A critical review of stage models, *Review of Educational Research*, 76, pp. 383–412.

Davies, B. (2003) Death to Critique and Dissent? The policies and practices of new managerialism and of 'evidence-based practice', *Gender and Education*, 15, pp. 91–103.

Davies, B. (2005) The (Im)possibility of Intellectual Work in Neoliberal Regimes, *Discourse: Studies in the Cultural Politics of Education*, 26, pp. 1–14.

De Ruyter, D. & Conroy, J. (2002) The Formation of Identity: The importance of ideals, *Oxford Review of Education*, 28, pp. 509–522.

Dreyfus, H. L. & Dreyfus, S. E. (1986) *Mind over Machine: The power of human intuition and expertise in the era of the computer* (New York, Free Press).

Gray, J. G. (1968) Introduction, in: M. Heidegger (ed.), *What is Called Thinking?* (New York, Harper & Row).

Grosz, E. (1994) *Volatile Bodies: Toward a corporeal feminism* (St Leonards, NSW, Allen & Unwin).

Grosz, E. (2004) *The Nick of Time: Politics, evolution and the untimely* (Crow's Nest, NSW, Allen & Unwin).

Heidegger, M. (1962/1927) *Being and Time*, trans. J. Macquarrie & E. Robinson (New York, SCM Press.)

Heidegger, M. (1998/1967) Plato's Doctrine of Truth, trans. T. Sheehan, in: W. McNeill (ed.), *Pathmarks* (Cambridge, Cambridge University Press), pp. 155–182.

Merleau-Ponty, M. (1962/1945) *Phenomenology of Perception* (London, Routledge & Kegan Paul).

Thomson, I. (2001) Heidegger on Ontological Education, or: How we become what we are, *Inquiry*, 44, pp. 243–268.

Thomson, I. (2004) Heidegger's Perfectionist Philosophy of Education in *Being and Time*, *Continental Philosophy Review*, 37, pp. 439–467.

Webster-Wright, A. (2006) *Understanding Continuing Professional Learning*. Unpublished PhD thesis, University of Queensland, Australia.

6

The Potentiality of Authenticity in Becoming a Teacher

Angus Brook

Introduction

This chapter arises out of the transition from a PhD thesis on Heidegger's phenomenology to my attempts to use phenomenology as a way of coming to terms with
becoming a teacher. The chapter will contain two avenues of exploration; the first
providing an interpretation of the phenomenon of education in Heideggerian
terms, the second attempting to show how Heidegger's phenomenology might
be constituted as a lived experience of teaching. The general aim of this chapter,
as such, is to move from a purely theoretical Heideggerian exposition of the
phenomenon of education to a way of applying this exposition to the practices
of teaching.

In this chapter I will argue that the key to the possibility of a lived experience of
being a teacher in a Heideggerian sense revolves around the notion of authenticity.
Herein, the notion of authenticity will be used to disclose the meaning of education
in terms of being human, and moreover, as the entrance point to the possibility
of a phenomenological interpretative engagement with the practices of teaching.
This argument will contain four sections: (S1) a brief overview of Heidegger's
phenomenology, (S2) a phenomenological interpretation of education, (S3) the
notion of authenticity and the phenomenon of teaching, and (S4) phenomenological
reflections on authenticity in the lived experience of teaching. In this final
section I will argue that a phenomenological interpretation of education might
be lived out as the foundation of, and teleological orientation towards, the
practices of teaching. I will utilise my own phenomenological reflections on the
practice of teaching during a Graduate Diploma in Education to supplement
this argument.

1. Heidegger's Phenomenology

I will, for the sake of clarity and brevity, avoid the more complex themes of
Heidegger's phenomenology and instead outline three main themes as a way into
a phenomenological interpretation of teaching/learning.[1] These themes will be:
ontology, de-construction, and the primordial characteristics of being-human.

Ontology

The easiest way of explaining Heidegger's phenomenology as a way of interpretation is through ontology: the study of the being of beings (entities). Being, for
Heidegger, means the ground of the ways an entity can be, or, 'being is always the
being of an entity' (Heidegger, 1962). With respect to teaching, then, the question
phenomenology begins with is: who is the entity that grounds teaching/learning as
a possibility? In other words, what is it about being-human that makes learning
(and thus teaching) a possible way of being?

A phenomenological interpretation of education is thus founded on the presupposition that teaching/learning is an expression of the being of humans which
shows itself through our everyday existence. This showing itself, however, is only
given insofar as we first understand how learning is founded upon being human;
by drawing out the hidden ground and meaning of the phenomenon of learning
(Heidegger, 1962). The primary aim of a phenomenological interpretation of
education is therefore to disclose how learning is an essential characteristic of the
being of humans and further, providing an ontological description of the primary
characteristics of the being of humans that makes learning (and therein teaching)
an existential possibility.

De-Construction

Heidegger's notion of de-construction tends to be less well-known than Derrida's
practice of deconstruction. This is somewhat ironic for a scholar of Heidegger
insofar as Derrida's coining of the term 'deconstruction' originated in Derrida's
translation of Heidgger's use of the term *Abbau*, a synonym of *De-struktion* (Iain
Thomson, 2000). Derrida's notion of deconstruction is thus arguably a derivative
philosophical practice founded on Heidegger's thinking about the question of being
and the problems of metaphysics combined with new ways of reading philosophical
texts founded upon post-structuralist linguistics; '*a hermeneutic semiology* (founded
upon the notion of) *differance*' (Silverman, 1994, pp. 20–21). This synthesis of
phenomenology and semiology is especially evident in Derrida's 1968 address to
the French Philosophical Society in which *differance* is posited as a way of re-reading
(deconstructing) the αρχε with regard to both ontology and post-structuralist
linguistics (Derrida, 1982). Let us then return to the theme of de-construction in
Heidegger's phenomenology.

Heidegger's phenomenology, as an interpretative approach to phenomena, is
mostly aptly called 'de-construction'. De-construction outlines the three phases of
phenomenology as a method: destruction, formal indication, and construction
(Heidegger, 1988). Phenomenology, as a hermeneutical method, begins with the
presupposition that we as humans always initially tend to misinterpret ourselves
insofar as we view ourselves as merely present; as a thing, physical or experienced,
i.e. through the attempt to 'know' the world (Heidegger, 1962). As such, the first
phase of phenomenological interpretation is called destruction or 'destructuring'
(*Destruktion*); of destroying our everyday preconceptions about a phenomenon

(Heidegger, 1988). In relation to the being of teaching, then, a phenomenological interpretation will begin with a destructuring of the basic preconceptions about teaching as an idea, e.g. teaching content, learning outcomes, students as objects, etc ...

Formal indication is a somewhat complex and technical term in phenomenology that is geared towards moving the interpretation from beings to the being of entities as a phenomenon (Heidegger, 1988). To put it overly simplistically, formal indication signifies the process of determining what is left after the destruction of the misconceptions or misinterpretations of a phenomenon (Heidegger, 2004). In the case of a phenomenological interpretation of teaching/learning, then, we must ask: what characteristics show themselves as central, or remain 'fundamental' and 'primordial' after we clear away the preconceptions about teaching?

Construction takes what is formally indicated—that which shows itself as 'belonging-to' the being of the phenomenon—and 'discovers/uncovers' the ground of the phenomenon (Heidegger, 1988). Construction, as such, is the interpretation of the being of the phenomenon: the foundation or ground of the possibility of teaching/learning in being-human. With regard to teaching, the constructive phase involves the attempt to determine the characteristics of being-human that found teaching/learning. Furthermore, a construction aims to disclose what teaching/learning means in its belonging-to being-human.

The Primary Characteristics of Being-human

I will utilise Heidegger's already posited 'equiprimordial' characteristics of being-human as a way into this interpretation. Heidegger provides three interrelated characteristics of being-human. These characteristics are ontological, that is: they are foundational of the human awareness of existence and thus our understanding and experience of life. Heidegger's characterisation of being-human is somewhat analogous to archaeology insofar as he posits the characteristics of being-human within layers of dependency.

Heidegger calls the first 'primordial' characteristic of being-human 'concern' (*besorgen*)(Heidegger, 1962). Herein, Heidegger asserts that the closest, or most evident, character of being-human is our everyday life of concern: our 'dealings', manipulation of things, equipment, or sense of things in the world according to use value (Heidegger, 1962). This characterisation of being-human as concern, is to say that the most immediately accessible grasp of ourselves is founded on our needs—our daily bread; a concern for our existence in a tangible sense.

The second primordial characteristic is called care (*sorge*) (Arendt, 1996).[2] Care signifies that our concern is founded on our caring; what we care about in relation to life. The notion of care, as such, is a kind of life-interpretation (horizon) that grounds our sense of being-with others (Heidegger, 1962). Care is also called 'being for the sake of others' or solicitude (Heidegger, 1962). In other words, Heidegger is positing two arguments through the notion of care: (i) that care as a 'being-with' or a 'being-for-the-sake-of' is the ground of our concern, and (ii) that being-human is intrinsically a kind of awareness or there-ness (*Da-Sein*) that is interpretative; we relate to others and the world on the basis of having already interpreted the world.

The final characteristic of being-human is called 'comportment' or directedness.[3] This notion views the originary ground or foundational characteristic of our being as a directedness towards 'ground' in general: the ground of our being or the ground of the meaning and sense of our existence (Heidegger, 1997). Comportment is thus the basic ground of being-human; a 'towards that which' grounds our own existence.

For Heidegger, this notion of comportment leads to what he calls an 'equiprimordiality' of being which then 'shows itself' in two modalities: authenticity or inauthenticity (Heidegger, 1962). Authenticity signifies a 'truly being-human' or the genuine possibilities of being-human, while inauthenticity signifies a 'forgetting' of being-human or the 'unhomely' (*unheimisch*) (Heidegger, 1996b). Heidegger claims that the everyday way of being-human is inauthentic; of misinterpretation or misdirection; a concern for that which is not human (Heidegger, 1962). The traditional scientific method exemplifies the thinking of inauthenticity: science begins with the everyday existence of things and then abstracts or objectifies the phenomenon within the notion of causality or physical presence. This is precisely what Heidegger calls 'mere presence-at-hand', where everything is measured by its physical/experiential presence; quantification-qualification, objectification-subjectification ... (Heidegger, 1962)

Authenticity, on the other hand, is constituted via the notion of being-one's-self, or becoming truly human; of caring for the sake of others and of being directed towards the ground of the sense/meaning of our life as humans (Heidegger, 1962). Equally, Heidegger constitutes authenticity as an interpretative relationship with death (mortality) and time (Heidegger, 1962). Herein, authenticity signifies the engagement with ones ownmost possibility (death) which therein founds the human sense of temporality (παρουσια); the anticipation of potentialities of being—of being or not being (Heidegger, 1962). The authentic, as such, is an engagement with existence that constitutes temporality in relation to anticipatory moments of becoming, and moreover, a resolution towards death as the final becoming of being human (Heidegger, 1962).

2. Heidegger on Teaching/Learning

Heidegger's characterisation of being-human not only gives us a sense of the ground of teaching/learning in relation to being-human, but also gives us the all-important foundation for a determination of the authentic/inauthentic modes of teaching/learning. I will address these themes in the discussion that follows.

The Interpretation of Education as Formation

In his lecture on 'Plato's Doctrine of Truth', Heidegger uses the metaphor of the cave as a way of providing a phenomenological interpretation of teaching/learning. Here, Heidegger interprets Plato's term paideia (παιδεια) as '*bildung*' (education/

formation) (Heidegger, 1998). Heidegger argues that what we call education is properly or authentically a formation of the human character that is guided by a principle/ground, i.e. being-human (Heidegger, 1998). Education is thus a leading the whole human back to who we are, or, a becoming truly human (Heidegger, 1998).

Heidegger then expands this notion of education as becoming genuinely human via an interpretation of Plato's dialogue. First, Heidegger argues that formation (education) is not 'pouring knowledge into the psyche as if it were some empty container', (Heidegger, 1998, p. 167) but rather, the trans-formation of our (inauthentic) self-understanding through a confrontation with our own being and what is authentic/proper/good in relation to our living (Heidegger, 1998). This formation is necessary, Heidegger and Plato argue, insofar as we begin life un(in)formed (Heidegger, 1998).

Heidegger then outlines the 'way of becoming' of education as disclosed by Plato: (i) un(in)formed—chained to presence/appearances, (ii) becoming aware of the question of our ground, (iii) moving out of the cave via a confrontation with the ground that transforms us, and then (iv) returning to the cave to care for others—to free others (Heidegger, 1998). Authentic education, as such, is being a learner in such a way that we become teachers (carers); we become humans who authentically care for others and the formation of others as authentic human beings.

Formation and Development

Heidegger's notion of formation is distinct from the notion of development often used in educational theory. Herein, the notion of development is both ontical and biological in character; as an account of physiological and cognitive phases of change within the growth of humans as biological organisms (Marsh, 2004; Snowman & Biehler, 2006). Thus, in the notion of development, it is presupposed that teachers design their learning activities, content, and teaching in such a way that they meet with the cognitive and physiological chronology of the students.

The notion of formation (or *bildung*) is an ontological and teleological concept. Initially, formation is an ontological concept insofar as it is founded on Aristotle's claim that the human being is the being who may always also be otherwise than it is (Aristotle, 1984b). Herein, the being of humans is such that we begin (and tend to remain) uninformed of our own potentiality for being. The notion of formation, as such, focuses on the possibility that a human individual may overcome our lack of formation.

Likewise, the notion of formation is onto-teleological in both an Aristotelian and Platonic sense. For Plato, formation (παιδεια) signifies the process of recovering the being of humans from forgetfulness, or, the recovery of the ideas (Plato, 1997). For Aristotle, the notion of formation is teleological in the sense of becoming a good human; or of becoming virtuous (Aristotle, 1984a). In both, formation signifies a life-long goal of becoming which is intrinsic to humans in our being (thinking being).

For Heidegger, formation is a phenomenon that belongs to the possibility of being truly human or authentically human, and therein, the possibility of disclosing the truth of being (Heidegger, 1998). Formation, Heidegger argues, signifies becoming truly human; a becoming that may be thrown upon us, may be taught to us, and that must always be chosen by us. In the first instance, Heidegger frequently argues that the ground of becoming truly human is often thrust upon humans via existential crisis or hardship (Heidegger, 1962). Like Aristotle, Heidegger argues that the formation of authenticity originates in such phenomena as leisure and wonder (Aristotle, 1984a), boredom (Heidegger, 1995), or anxiety (Heidegger, 1962), which destroy our sense of everydayness and confront us with the question of our own potentialities for being.

Equally, the foundation of becoming authentic may be teaching, as illustrated by Heidegger's commentary of the allegory of the cave. Herein, teaching founds becoming authentic only insofar as teaching serves as a deconstruction of everydayness; confronting students with the preconceptions and inauthenticity of everyday life, leading the student to the question of their own being.

Finally, the foundation of becoming authentic is freedom. Freedom, Heidegger argues, actually signifies the freedom to ground and to be the ground (Heidegger, 1929; Heidegger, 2002). The notion of freedom, as such, returns to the determination of the being of humans as that being who may always also be otherwise than itself. For, becoming authentic in the Heideggerian sense is the human freedom to choose how we interpret or relate to temporality, and ultimately our deaths, in such a way that we find or lose our sense of being; that we become truly human or remain un(in)formed of our ground (Heidegger, 2002).

3. Authenticity and the Phenomenon of Teaching

Heidegger formulates education in its proper sense as the formation of authenticity. In this respect authenticity signifies being truly human; which is the genuine or proper *telos* of human existence. However, Heidegger also claims that humans have a primordial tendency to fall away from our own being, or, that our everyday way of existence is to not be ourselves (Heidegger, 1962). As such, the primary meaning of authenticity is becoming; a towards which or goal of human existence. Herein, Heidegger constitutes authenticity as a problem of the potentiality for being truly human and thus, a question of how this potentiality is possible.

Heidegger then proposes phenomenology as a way into this becoming authentic. Phenomenology is formulated as a way of questioning and interpreting that gives access to an understanding of the meaning of the truth of being human, i.e. authenticity. However, Heidegger also posits phenomenology in itself as a way of being; as a way of becoming authentic (Heidegger, 1999). As such, phenomenology is constituted as an authentic way of existence, or, a lived experience of becoming truly human (Heidegger, 1999). When we turn to the notion of authenticity and the phenomenon of teaching, it follows that a phenomenological interpretation of education should also be possible to live as an interpretative praxis.

Authenticity and Teaching

The phenomenological interpretation of education discloses the teacher as a human being with an extraordinary task. For, the teacher is a human like any other (with the tendency to fall away from being truly human), and yet, has the task of cultivating and building the formation of others. This becoming of teaching contains at least two primary characteristics.

Initially, the becoming of teachers can be characterised as that of being exemplary learners (Thomson, 2001). Teachers must be humans that exemplify learning (in terms of formation) as a way of being; so that students are shown learning and can see how learning works as a way of life. Herein, learning is more than the curriculum taught, but is additionally the formation of being truly human in general. The teacher as an exemplary learner is thus a human whose life discloses the authentic possibilities of human existence. Therefore, insofar as there are many expressions of authentic potentialities for being human, the teacher also discloses the authentic possibilities of being human as expressed through different curriculum subjects.

The second characteristic of the becoming of teachers can be called being ethical. This is a somewhat controversial claim insofar as Heidegger opposed ethics as a discipline (Heidegger, 1946), and yet, the ethical is an intrinsic dimension of Heidegger's notion of authenticity. To explain briefly: Heidegger rejected the philosophical discipline of ethics on the grounds that ethics has always constituted the good as something extrinsic to being human, e.g. God, or as something ontical, e.g. knowledge of human action (humanism). Heidegger claims that ethics is thus invalid insofar as it does not and cannot address the question of the truth of being human (Heidegger, 1946). However, the alternative of seeking the truth of being, Heidegger argues, is not ethics but rather ontology (Heidegger, 1946). Nonetheless, I would propose that insofar as authenticity is constituted as the *telos* of human existence, i.e. 'the ought' of being human, authenticity will pose an ethical dilemma for the practices of teaching.

The ethical character of the practices of teachers arises precisely in the potentiality of the lived experience of authentic teaching. The possibility of living out a phenomenological interpretation of education poses the question of an interpretative praxis of teaching that is authentic. As such, this possibility poses for teachers an ethical dilemma of authenticity. As Heidegger states, the being of teaching is ultimately for the sake of others as the authentic caring for students; of a becoming truly human for others and for the sake of the formation of authenticity in others (Heidegger, 1998). Therefore, the being ethical of a teacher can be constituted as the intrinsic goal of the teacher to care for the authenticity of students. This is precisely the goal of teaching that characterises the extraordinary task of teaching.

We have arrived at a point in which the foundations of the being/becoming of teaching (in a Heideggerian sense) have been disclosed. Herein, the primary problem of the possibility of living out phenomenology as an interpretative praxis of teaching has been disclosed through the question of authenticity. In the next section, I will suggest just a few possible determinations of how this authentic interpretative praxis of being a teacher might be lived.

4. Phenomenological Reflections on Authenticity in the Lived Experience of Teaching

The problem of 'applying' a phenomenological interpretation of the phenomenon of education centres on the question of whether an ontological understanding of authenticity might serve as a foundation for determinate practices of teaching, and moreover, whether there are dimensions of authenticity that might inform the goals of teaching as a practice. In this final section of the chapter, I will discuss five themes in relation to the practices of teaching that are founded upon dimensions of authenticity and that could serve as a way of building/cultivating the goal of authenticity in students.

Planning for Authenticity

Heidegger argues that authenticity is the goal of human existence. Insofar as humans are neither born authentic nor 'naturally' authentic, authenticity is something cultivated or built within existence. Heidegger argues that there is a blueprint or architectural plan for human authenticity, namely: being (Heidegger, 1993). The phenomenological interpretation of being human is intended to disclose precisely this ground, foundation, or blueprint for authenticity. As such, the first dimension of the becoming/being of teaching might be called something like 'planning for authenticity'. This planning would serve as an interpretative praxis where the teacher utilises a phenomenological understanding of being human to serve as the ground of and goal orientation (τελοσ) for teaching. Moreover, planning is a determinate activity of teaching through which a phenomenological interpretation of education may be applied.

Planning is a dominant theme of the everyday practices of teaching. Planning can provide a misleading sense of security insofar as planning easily falls into thinking about teaching as teaching content. Here, the security of having planned content to teach could easily lead to a lack of thought about the 'how' of teaching and the 'how' of building an authentic learning environment. Some of the questions that arise are: can we plan for authenticity? Can we plan so that outcomes and content are central without being essential? Can we plan to incorporate authenticity as the foundation of teaching/learning that emerge through the content and outcomes?

I would argue that planning for authentic learning environments may be constituted as a kind of authentic relationship with students. Herein, planning can become a more flexible way of preparing for an authentic learning environment. A time for the teacher to think about our relationship with students that is responsive to the learning environment that has already formed, while also looking forward to how the learning environment can be built in more authentic ways. Planning, as such, can be a phenomenological interpretation of the authentic/inauthentic character of the learning environment which looks to building a more authentic learning environment in the future.

Formation and Dwelling

Heidegger argues that a central characteristic of authenticity is ethos or dwelling (Heidegger, 2005). The notion of dwelling posits that an essential characteristic of authenticity is 'homeliness' or being oneself in our environment (Heidegger, 2005). As such, the goal of becoming truly human is intrinsically connected to building or cultivating this sense of being human in our environment; of being at home with and as ourselves in the world. For the teacher, the notion of dwelling incorporates two goals: the building of an environment in which students are given space to be themselves (in relation to formation) and the cultivation of an environment that assists students in becoming truly human.

In this respect, the school is a place of dwelling (Heidegger, 2002) that forms the potential ways of being of the students (Ream & Ream, 2005). For teachers, building a learning environment for students will not be authentic unless teachers first grasp what it means for humans to dwell (Ream & Ream, 2005). In other words, the school, classroom, or learning environment is a place in which students and teachers live, and thus, should have a sense of dwelling (being ourselves) in the school (Ream & Ream, 2005). An authentic learning environment, it can be argued, is one in which the teacher creates an environment that inspires and cultivates the formation of students as authentic human beings (Ream & Ream, 2005).

One possibility of applying the notion of dwelling could be called 'making room for authenticity' in the classroom. This theme can be viewed in three interrelated ways. First, making room for authenticity could be used to allow or encourage a sense of ownership through the provision of choice about the 'how' of learning and how the room is set up. Equally, the teacher could attempt to foster opportunities for participation, especially encouraging students to engage in teaching, communal writing, and communal learning. Another way to make room for authenticity could be through questioning and discussion. In this, the teacher could build an authentic learning environment by making room for the students' own personal questions and thoughts about what is being thought about.

Another application of the notion of dwelling could be called the possibility of building authentic learning environments on the basis of showing students other ways of being. In this, the teacher could provide an environment through questioning and role-playing that provokes a sense of other ways of being. An important dimension of building an authentic learning environment, in this sense, would be the cultivation of learning through provoking a sense of being what is learned about.

The Formation of Authentic Relations

The third theme can be called the formation of authentic relations. In *Being and Time*, Heidegger maintains that the truth of being human is care (*sorge*) (Heidegger, 1962). Care is both an interpretative horizon (how we interpret our relations with others) and a goal of being-with in an authentic sense. In the same way, the practice of teaching should pursue the formation of an interpretative horizon of care within students' awareness of life that will cultivate in students the goal of caring relations. This doubled practice of care in teaching can be called the formation of authentic relations. There are two primary ways of constituting care as the foundation of forming authentic relations: the first with regard to becoming truly human in general, and the second in terms of caring relationships. Both can be viewed as ethical dimensions of attempts to implement Heidegger's phenomenology.

In the first instance the phenomenon of teaching, in an authentic sense, can be constituted as a question of ethical relations; of being-with students that discloses who we are as humans in our potential for good (Thomson, 2001). Authentic or ethical education requires that the teacher-student relation serves as a basis for confronting ourselves and our living (ετηοσ—our authentic possibilities) (Thomson, 2001). The teacher-student relationship is thus, in the first case, the practice of ethical formation in relation to the question of what it is to be human.

Equally, the formation of authentic relations can be constituted via a personal sense of the ethical wherein the teacher veers away from treating students as '*vorhanden* (merely present at hand), that is, as theoretically constituted objects ...' (Donnelly, 1999, p. 946). Rather, teaching as the formation of authentic relations is first and foremost an ethical relation of being-with (Donnelly, 1999). Authentic teaching, as such, consists of a relation with students that renders the teachers 'care' and 'concern' for the students transparent (Donnelly, 1999). In other words, teaching becomes the formation of authentic relations insofar as the teachers demonstrate, explain, and genuinely live out their 'care' for students and their concern for the formation of students.

The Formation of Questioning/Thinking

A central dimension of Heidegger's notion of authenticity is the formation of thinking (Heidegger, 1968; Heidegger, 2005). Heidegger calls thinking, and language in which thinking shows itself, the house of being (Heidegger, 1968). In this, thinking and questioning do not simply mean the ability to think, or even the formation of thinking skills, e.g. logic, rhetoric, critical thinking or analysis. Rather, thinking and questioning refers to an awareness of what is worth thinking about (Heidegger, 1968; Heidegger, 1980), and further, the formation of the ability to ask the right questions. For humans, Heidegger argues, there is only one question, one matter for thinking, upon which all other questions are founded: the question of the meaning of being human (Heidegger, 1962). This question is the foundational question for humans, not simply in the possibility of disclosing our own sense of being, but also insofar as this question founds all other questions, e.g. how we know, how we experience the world, how we constitute meaning, how we decide upon actions, and so on. It is, in part, the task of the teacher to cultivate and build this ability to think, and in thinking, ask the right questions. It is the role of the teacher to show students how to think and therein lead the students to ask genuine/authentic questions about their existence. A dimension of the role of teachers in this respect is the formation of de-constructive thinking; of leading the student from their everyday preconceptions about existence back to the question of their being. Further, the teacher needs to guide students back from the question of being into their own lives; building a space in which the students may question and think about how to constitute their own existence. The formation of thinking and questioning, as Heidegger argues, takes place solely for the sake of living and for the sake of deliberations about how to live (Heidegger, 1999).

Regional Ontology and the Formation of Student Potentialities for Being

An important aspect of Heidegger's philosophy is the notion of regional ontology, or, the plurality of the expressions of being human in existence. Herein, Heidegger's fundamental ontology (Heidegger, 1962) seeks to uncover/discover the sense of being human in general. This in turn founds the possibility of explicating regional ontologies, for example, for the ontical sciences such as natural science, technology, history, theology, the humanities, and so on, in terms of how they are grounded upon the being of humans. Every regional ontology is founded upon: a) an interpretation of being human in general, and b) on an interpretation of how that particular science is an expression or potentiality of human existence. In the same way, we can say that the lived experience of teaching will engage with the possibility of the students' authentic becoming, or formation, through a phenomenological interpretation of curriculum subjects as expressions of regional ontology.

For teaching, curriculum subjects are correlates of regional ontologies, i.e. each subject is founded on being human and expresses a potentiality for being in human existence. Therefore, each subject not only discloses something about human existence, but also provides a basis for the students to grasp the authentic potentialities for their own existence. For example, history can teach us about how humans have interpreted life, thought about a good life, how our society has arrived at the views that are dominant today, and the ethical dilemmas that arise herein. Science can help us think about the human relation to the physical/natural world and how this relation could be better. For example, Health/Physical Education can help us think about our physical/mental well-being and the well-being of others. Finally, the study of religion can help students understand how humans interpret the meaning of life as a whole and also help students to think about the purpose/meaning of their own lives.

Conclusion

A Heideggerian phenomenological interpretation of education provides the foundation for a philosophical approach to teaching/learning in which the understanding and explication of being human is given priority. Equally, a phenomenological interpretation of education provides the philosophical foundation for determining the general ground and goal of teaching as the formation of authenticity. Ultimately, Heidegger intended phenomenology to transcend a theoretical understanding of a phenomenon in constituting an authentic interpretative praxis. In this regard, the chapter has outlined just a few possible ways in which an authentic interpretative praxis might be instigated. Heidegger's notion of authenticity, however, contains such rich possibilities for thinking about teaching practices that this chapter could only ever hope to scratch the surface. Some other possibilities have been suggested, such as: education as becoming who we are (Thomson, 2001), a way of interpreting learning environments (Ream & Ream, 2005), being a teacher (Donnelly, 1999), poetic learning (Pike, 2003), learning through existential crisis (Segal, 1999), and authenticity and information and communication technologies (Lambeir, 2002; Peters, 2003).

I will conclude with a brief synopsis of four primary themes which arise out of a Heideggerian phenomenological interpretation of education:

1. Learning signifies the questioning of what it is to be human, or, who we are as humans: our past, our relation to the world we live in, our potentialities for being, and our relation to other humans.
2. To learn about being human also requires that we learn how to think and communicate our thinking to others. This is founded, in the first instance, on a familiarity with thinking; that we learn what is worth thinking about. Further, to learn how to think requires that we learn how to ask questions and the various ways of interpreting what we find.
3. Learning is primarily learning about meaning, or, how to go about living life. As such, it is arguable that the most important dimension of learning is that of learning about being human in such a way that we learn how to think about the meaning of life; of who we are as humans.
4. Learning is thinking for the sake of being human that we may become the potential we have for authenticity as humans. Becoming or being an authentic teacher, as such, is becoming in such a way that the authentic possibilities of being-human show themselves through the formation of learning.

Notes

1. For those interested in the more complex themes of Heidegger's phenomenology, I would recommend Heidegger's *Being and Time* (1962 or 1996a), *Basic Problems of Phenomenology* (1988), *Basic Writings* (1993/2002), and *Pathmarks* (1998).
2. This is a German translation of the Latin '*caritas*'—love for the other (see Arendt, 1996, p. 18).
3. This is Heidegger's version of Husserl's term 'intentionality'.

References

Arendt, H. (1996) *Love and Saint Augustine* (Chicago, The University of Chicago Press).
Aristotle (1984a) Nichomachean Ethics, in: J. Barnes (ed.), *The Complete Works of Aristotle* (Princeton, NJ, Princeton University Press).
Aristotle (1984b) The Metaphysics, in: J. Barnes (ed.), *The Complete Works of Aristotle* (Princeton, NJ, Princeton University Press).
Derrida (1982) *Margins of Philosophy*, A. Bass, trans. (Chicago, The University of Chicago Press).
Donnelly, J. F. (1999) Schooling Heidegger: On being in teaching, *Teaching and Teacher Education*, 15, pp. 933–949.
Heidegger, M. (1929) The Concept of Ground, in: W. McNeill (ed.), *Pathmarks* (Cambridge, Cambridge University Press).
Heidegger, M. (1946) Letter on Humanism, in: W. McNeill (ed.), *Pathmarks* (Cambridge, Cambridge University Press, 1998).
Heidegger, M. (1962) *Being and Time*, J. Macquarrie & E. Robinson, trans. (New York, Harper & Row).
Heidegger, M. (1968) *What is Called Thinking?* J. G. Gray, trans. (London, Harper & Row).

Heidegger, M. (1980) *An Introduction to Metaphysics*, R. Manheim, trans. (New Haven, Yale University Press).

Heidegger, M. (1988) *The Basic Problems of Phenomenology*, A. Hofstadter, trans. (Bloomington, Indiana University Press).

Heidegger, M. (1993) 'Building, Dwelling, Thinking', in: D. Farrell Krell (ed.), *Basic Writings* (London, Routledge).

Heidegger, M. (1995) *Fundamental Concepts of Metaphysics*, W. McNeill & N. Walker, trans. (Bloomington, Indiana University Press).

Heidegger, M. (1996a) *Being and Time: A translation of Sein und Zeit*, J. Stambaugh, trans. (Albany, State University of New York Press).

Heidegger, M. (1996b) *Holderlin's Hymn 'The Ister'*, W. McNeill & J. Davis, trans. (Bloomington, Indiana University Press).

Heidegger, M. (1997) Phenomenological Interpretations with Respect to Aristotle: Indications of the hermeneutical situation, *Man and World*, 30, p. 4.

Heidegger, M. (1998) Plato's Doctrine of Truth, in: W. McNeill (ed.), *Pathmarks* (Cambridge, Cambridge University Press).

Heidegger, M. (1999) *Ontology: The hermeneutics of facticity*, J. van Buren, trans. (Bloomington, Indiana University Press).

Heidegger, M. (2002) Building, Dwelling, Thinking, in: D. F. Krell (ed.), *Basic Writings* (London, Routledge).

Heidegger, M. (2004) An Introduction to the Phenomenology of Religion, *The Phenomenology of Religious Life*, M. Fritsch & J. A. Gosetti-Ferencei, trans. (Bloomington, Indiana University Press).

Heidegger, M. (2005) *The Essence of Human Freedom*, T. Sadler, trans. (London, Continuum).

Lambeir, B. (2002) Comfortably Numb in the Digital Era: Man's being as standing-reserve or dwelling silently, in: M. A. Peters (ed.), *Heidegger, Education, and Modernity* (Lanham, MD, Rowman & Littlefield Publishers).

Marsh, C. (2004) *Becoming a Teacher: Knowledge, skills and issues* (Sydney, Pearson Education Australia).

Peters, M. (2003) Technologising Pedagogy: The Internet, nihilism, and phenomenology of learning, *Simile*, 3, p. 1.

Pike, M. (2003) On Being in English Teaching: A time for Heidegger? *Changing English*, 10, p. 1.

Plato (1997) Republic, in: J. M. Cooper (ed.), *Complete Works* (Indianapolis, IN, Hackett Publishing Company).

Ream, T. C. & Ream, T. W. (2005) From Low-Lying Roofs to Towering Spires: Toward a Heideggerian understanding of learning environments, *Educational Philosophy and Theory*, 37, p. 4.

Segal, S. (1999) The Existential Conditions of Explicitness: An Heideggerian perspective, *Studies in Continuing Education*, 21, p. 1.

Silverman, H. J. (1994) *Textualities: Between hermeneutics and deconstruction* (New York, Routledge).

Snowman, J. & Biehler, R. (2006) *Psychology Applied to Teaching* (11th edn.) (Boston, Houghton Mifflin Company).

Thomson, I. (2000) Ontotheology? Understanding Heidegger's *Destruktion* of metaphysics, *International Journal of Philosophical Studies*, 8, p. 3.

Thomson, I. (2001) Heidegger on Ontological Education, or: How we become what we are, *Inquiry*, 44, p. 2.

7

Transition into High School: A phenomenological study

KRISHNAVENI GANESON & LISA C. EHRICH

Introduction

Transition is a process of moving from the known to the unknown (Green, 1997) and transition from primary school to high school can be described in this way. In Australia, there is a two tiered system of primary and secondary schooling operating where school students typically undergo at least two transitions. Firstly, when they leave home to attend pre-school/primary school; and secondly, when they leave primary school to enter secondary school. Potentially some students may experience up to four transitions: from home to kindergarten to pre-school to primary school to secondary school while for a smaller number of students who attend P-12 schools, there may be only one transition: from home to preschool.

The particular focus in this study lies with students' experience of starting high school because the movement from primary to secondary is said to be an important milestone in their lives (Legters & Kerr, 2001). It is a time that coincides with adolescent developmental changes including physical, cognitive, emotional and psychological changes. It is a time when students can face social, curriculum and peer challenges (La Rue, Raymond & Weiss, 2004) such as the fear of being bullied (Cormack, 1991; Cumming & Cormack, 1996; Kiloh & Morris, 2000; Akos, 2002), friendship (Green, 1997; Hinebauch, 2002; Cauley & Jovanovich, 2006) and identity issues (Gattis, 1995; Kaplan, 1996; Elias, 2002; Walker, 2002). Moreover, adolescents can sometimes fear becoming lost in the new environment of the high school (Kaplan, 1996) or find the new academic challenges too rigorous (Hatton, 1995).

It appears that the growing body of literature concerning student transition from primary school to high school has been based largely on academic and practitioners' views on childhood development and the developmental needs of children. That there is limited empirical work in this field (Luke *et al.*, 2003) demonstrates a need for further examination of this area. For this reason, this study explores the phenomenon of the transition into secondary school from the lived experiences of sixteen students from one government school in New South Wales who entered high school for the first time in 2005.

The chapter begins by reviewing some of the salient research and writing in the field of transition into high school. It does this by locating the issue of transition within the broader field of the middle years literature. It then makes an argument for the suitability and relevance of phenomenological psychology as a methodology to uncover students' experiences of starting high school. The next part of the chapter presents the findings—seven essential themes and their general descriptions which emerged from the students' experiences, and arising from themes is a discussion of key issues and implications for practice.

Transition into High School

Since the 1990s, there has been a resurgence of interest in the provision of education for early adolescents (Carrington, 2006). This has been evident by a plethora of policies and programs targeting students in the 'middle years' age group (i.e. students between the ages of 10 and 15 years) (Pendergast, 2005). Much of this early middle years research focused on transitional difficulties faced by students as they moved from primary to secondary schools (Carrington, 2006). Some of this research showed that students' experiences of transition influenced their educational success (Barratt, 1998; Dockett & Perry, 1999a,b, 2001, 2003; Early, Pianta & Cox, 1999). Furthermore, it was found that schools that had little emphasis on ways to ease transition tended to have higher failure and dropout rates among their high school students than those that had specific programs to ease transition (Legters & Kerr, 2001).

In recognition of the difficulties faced by early adolescents, the Education Department in New South Wales' response has been to focus on transition as a key platform of middle years reform, and to provide a range of support materials for teachers to use to facilitate student learning (Luke *et al.*, 2003; Carrington, 2006). Other education departments and schooling systems in Australia have responded in other ways. For example, middle years reform has been a key priority for the Victorian Department of Education and Training where it has implemented a myriad of significant projects focusing on literacy and numeracy as well as developing school action plans and gaining tri-sectoral (i.e. Government, Catholic and Independent schools) commitment to the middle years program (Luke *et al.*, 2003).

In more recent times, a new agenda of middle years reform has emerged. Central to this 'middle schooling' agenda are a range of educational issues endeavouring to provide more responsive and engaging curriculum and pedagogy for students to help them function in a changing world (Pendergast, 2005). Middle schooling is seen to be characterised by a set of effective school practices involving an integrated curriculum, teacher team work and collaboration, authentic outcomes based curriculum and assessment, and the development of students' higher order thinking and problem solving skills (Carrington, 2006). Yet revolving around the reform is the 'provision of a seamless transition from primary schooling (which is tradi-tionally student-centred) to secondary schooling (which is traditionally subject or discipline-centred) leading to more effective student learning, positive experiences in adolescence and a desire and capacity for lifelong learning' (Carrington, Pendergast, Bahr, Kapitzke, Mayer & Mitchell in Luke *et al.*, 2003, p. 25). Of interest to this study, then, is the phenomenon of students' experiences of transition into high school.

To date there is a sizeable body of research that has focused on student transitions (e.g. Cotterell, 1982; Arowosafe & Irvin, 1992; Kirkpatrick, 1992; Hatton, 1995; Yates, 1999; Dockett & Perry, 1999a,b, 2001, 2003; Johnstone, 2001, 2002; Akos, 2002; Dockett *et al.*, 2002). On closer scrutiny of this research, there appears to be little Australian research and limited phenomenological studies that have considered students' experiences of transition into secondary school as they live through the transitionary period. An exception here is the work of Akos (2002). Akos (2002) conducted a longitudinal study of student experiences in the United States using Giorgi's (1985a) phenomenological approach to arrive at themes relating to students' experience of transition. He also employed a quantitative approach in the second stage of data analysis to analyse his findings further. His study showed that students were predominantly concerned about school rules and procedures and most worried about older students. The positive aspects of transition included use of lockers, new friends, freedom and classes. His study suggested that transition yields more positive experiences for some students than negative. Other challenges that students face when making the transition from primary to secondary school are considered next.

Challenges Posed by Transition into High School

Discontinuity in peer relationships can affect some students entering high school for the first time. Students are regrouped for different subjects and this can cause anxiety about maintaining their peer relationships (Elias, 2002; Hinebauch, 2002). According to research carried out by Akos (2002) and Simmons and Blyth (1987), girls more so than boys experienced peer relationships as most stressful during transition. Girls worried about being bullied by other and bigger students more than boys did, whereas boys found peer relationships, conflict with authority and academic pressures as equal stressors (Akos, 2002). Kiloh and Morris (2000) reported that bullying is an issue for students during transition, and more so with low achieving students. Arowosafe and Irvin (1992) interviewed students leaving primary school in the USA about their stressors and found that students were stressed about safety concerns in the new school. Similarly, studies by Cumming and Cormack (1996), Hatton (1995), Mizelle (1999) and Mizelle and Irvin (2000) found that students seemed concerned by bullying and intimidation by older students when they enter high school.

Green (1997) conducted a study with 58 participants on the shift from primary and secondary school in Victoria, Australia, which demonstrated that these students found high school transition problematic. Although students did look forward to transition into secondary school, they faced social problems in adjusting to the new school and making friends. In a longitudinal study of students' experiences of shifting from primary to secondary school in Victoria, Yates (1999) noted that the 'sea of unknown faces was worse than students had first anticipated' (p. 28). Indeed, the socialisation process was seen to be an even bigger problem for those students who came from a primary school with a smaller enrolment. It appears that problems related to socialisation during transition will arise until students feel secure in their new school and they begin to feel secure when they start to make friends (Green, 1997).

Curricular/Academic Challenges

The changed curriculum to which the students are exposed when they enter high school can be a source of anxiety (Education Queensland, 2001; Meece, 2002). Students may now learn more subjects than previously, subjects tend not to be inter-disciplinary but compartmentalised and the amount of homework is intensified and given more frequently (Beane, 1991; Urdan, Midgley & Wood, 1995; Mullins & Irvin, 2000).

As Cotterell (2002) indicates, high schools favour a subject-based curriculum compared to a thematic, inter-disciplinary approach adopted in primary schools. In an Australian study of first year high school students conducted by Cumming and Cormack (1996), the subjects taught were not related to each other and were seen by the students to be disconnected and discrete. Similarly, Green's (1997) investigation of high school transition showed that students move from subject to subject without any integration in the curriculum between subjects. Students find this lack of integration between subjects and the compartmentalisation of subjects/ knowledge an additional challenge because they have little experience of subjects being taught as discrete units (Beane, 1991; Cumming, 1996). However, in more recent times, an important platform of a middle schooling reform movement has been a focus on improving both curriculum and pedagogy for young adolescents (Luke *et al.*, 2003). Here, an integrated and theme based approach to teaching and learning has been advocated as a means of overcoming the compartmentalised nature of work traditionally undertaken in high school subjects (Manning, 2000). Yet, such an approach poses considerable implications for the traditional model of secondary schooling characterised by several discipline specialist teachers operating in isolation from each other (Carrington, 2006).

Some students find the academic demands of homework too rigorous and too challenging (Hertzog & Morgan, 1998; Elias, 2002). Hatton (1995) interviewed students from Years 6 to 10 in a rural private girls' school in New South Wales about organisational structure and middle school. Her findings showed that students were unaccustomed to doing a great deal of homework which then placed considerable demands upon them academically. The lack of skills to complete homework affects students during transition because it is an additional issue that they have to overcome. Besides academic and curriculum challenges, students during transition have to get used to a new location, new school environment and organisation.

Geographic and Physical Challenges

When students enter high school they may move to a new geographic location, experience new school rules and a new organisational structure. This is the case in New South Wales, where primary schools and high schools are located on different campuses. Getting to know the physical location of the school has been identified as causing difficulty for students particularly in the early stages of entry to high school (Yates, 1999).

Apart from geographical location, many primary schools in New South Wales have a relatively smaller school enrolment than high schools (Department of Education and Training, 2003). The reality is that students moving from primary to high school have to get used to a larger physical size of a school (Hatton, 1995). Students fear being late to class, being lost and not being able to find lockers, canteens and classrooms. Studies conducted by Cotterell (1982), Green (1997), Johnstone (2002, 2001), Simmons and Blyth (1987) and Weldy (1990), reported that students are also anxious about organisational and geographic aspects of the new school. As an example, a qualitative study by Johnstone (2001) of a group of rural students who made the transition from primary into high school, identified adapting to the high school's organisational culture as a key concern. Organisational culture related to issues such as school size, layout and students finding their way around the school. Similarly, Hatton's (1995) study found that students were anxious about the size of the school. Her recommendation was that school sizes should be reduced to remove this anxiety.

Organisational Challenges

Students entering high schools are introduced to more complex organisational structures than those of primary schools. They are exposed to many teachers, with different expectations and standards. High school teachers teach a number of classes each day and a large number of students. Green's (1997) qualitative study of transition into high school found that students worry that their secondary teachers do not know them as well as their primary teachers. These students have less contact time with each teacher due to the organisational structure of high school and this has led them to believe that teachers are not always available when they are needed.

As well as the experience of feeling isolated and anonymous, students sometimes find high schools unfriendly and bureaucratic environments. Based on the literature reviewed, Legters and Kerr (2001) concluded that the large bureaucratic nature of most high schools offers little support for incoming students, especially those with weak social and academic preparation. Transition into high school can be made more difficult for some students when they are faced not only with an unfamiliar new environment (Tonkin & Watt, 2003) but also a less intimate and larger environment. Based on evidence of the aforementioned studies, transition into high school can be problematic for some students due to a range of social, peer, curriculum, academic, physical, geographic and organisational challenges. The next part of the chapter considers the methodology that steered this research study.

Methodology

The first part of this section discusses the nature of phenomenology, its philosophical roots and background information on phenomenological psychology. The second part discusses the data collection and analysis approach following Giorgi's phenomenological psychological methodology that guided the study.

Phenomenology: A Philosophy and Methodology

Phenomenology is both a philosophy and a methodology (Patton, 1990) and for this reason, much confusion surrounds the term. Phenomenology had its origins in the European tradition which emerged from the philosophy of Husserl, a late 19th century German mathematician who developed a philosophical phenomenology and a phenomenological psychology (Husserl, 1927/1971). Central to phenomenological philosophy are four key themes that Merleau-Ponty (1962) describes as the entrance to which we can access phenomenology. These are description, reduction, essences and intentionality. 'Description' in phenomenology is concerned with describing things as one experiences them. It means a turning away from science and scientific knowledge and returning to the 'things themselves' (Husserl, 1900/ 1970, p. 252). The consequence of doing this is to place a person's experience at the centre of any investigation. 'Reduction' or 'bracketing' refers to the need for individuals to temporarily suspend taken for granted assumptions and presuppositions about phenomena so the things themselves can be returned to (Merleau-Ponty, 1962). 'Essences' refer to the core meaning of an individual's experience of any given phenomenon that makes it what it is. 'Intentionality' refers to consciousness and that individuals are always conscious of something (Merleau-Ponty, 1962). 'Intentionality' is the total meaning of an object.

An important movement in psychology emerged in the late 1960s in the United States of America that endeavoured to marry psychology with insights from phenomenology. Psychologists who followed this movement incorporated some of Husserl's central concepts to establish a psychology as a distinctly human science (Giorgi, Fischer & von Eckartsberg, 1971) as well as drawing upon notions from existential phenomenology (Spinelli, 1989). Giorgi was one of the early psychologists to translate the phenomenological perspective into a scientific research methodology for psychology. He turned to Merleau-Ponty's four criteria and expressed these in ways helpful for phenomenological psychology. According to Giorgi (1985a), the aim of phenomenological psychological research is for subjects to describe fully their experiences. Subjects describe phenomena and the researcher is said to employ a reduction when he/she begins to analyse the descriptions (Giorgi, 1985a, p. 49). Phenomenological psychological studies seek general essences or essential structures which are context related. These structures make a thing what it is. Intentionality within a phenomenological psychological study maintains that there is an inseparable connectedness of the human being to the world (Giorgi, 1985a, pp. 50–51). Together these four themes constitute a core component of phenomenological psychology. A phenomenological psychological approach (following Giorgi, 1985a,b) was deemed appropriate to use in this study because it provides insights into understanding human experiences by producing accurate descriptions of these experiences while humans undergo and live through the experience.

Data Collection and Data Analysis

According to Tesch (1984), the appropriate number of participants in a phenomenological study depends upon the nature of the phenomenon to be researched. While Tesch (1984) has suggested that between 10 to 15 participants is usual, she also mentioned as few as six and as many as 25 participants have been used in phenomenological studies.

In this study, sixteen participants from one government school in New South Wales agreed to participate. Consistent with data collection methods pertinent for phenomenological psychological studies, participants were asked to describe their experiences and record these in journals. Students were given free reign to explore any experience they encountered as a result of being in high school and to record their entries at least three times in the first six weeks of high school and then at least twice in the remaining four weeks. Students were encouraged to provide insights into their experiences during this transitionary period in high school. The data were collected for the first ten weeks of the term since this time was considered the crucial period of transition. The journals were collected at the end of each week and returned immediately to students after being photocopied. At the end of the tenth week all journals were collected for the final time and analysis commenced.

The journal entries became the sole source of data and were analysed following Giorgi's (1985b, pp. 11–18) four step process for phenomenological psychological research studies:

1. *Reading the entire description to get a sense of the whole statement.*
   The researcher reads the journal entries to get a sense of the whole experience written by participants.
2. *Discrimination of meaning units within a psychological perspective.*
   The researcher reads the descriptions and identifies meaning units. A meaning unit is described as words and phrases which express clearly a meaning which distinguishes it from other meanings.
3. *Transformation of subjects' everyday expressions into psychological language with emphasis on the phenomenon being investigated.*
   The researcher transforms the participants' colloquially expressed language into more meaningful and revealing psychological language.
4. *Synthesis of transformed meaning units into a consistent statement of the structure of the experience being investigated.*
   The researcher works to synthesise and tie the meaning units together into a descriptive statement of essential, non-redundant psychological meanings using two steps.

The first step involves the researcher developing a situated structural description for each experience; and an additional step is required to produce a single general structural description that represents the total experience of the phenomenon (Giorgi, 1985b, pp. 10–19). As can be seen above, the first three steps are not greatly different from other types of qualitative research; the main difference lies in the nature of the data—concrete lived experience rather than participants' reflections, opinions and analysis. Unique to phenomenological psychological research is step 4 that requires the researcher to firstly rewrite a specific statement in third person which depicts the experience and, secondly, to write a general statement which synthesises all of the specific statements (Ehrich, 1998).

Journal entries for students were examined very carefully. As was expected, not all students wrote three journal entries every week during the ten week period. However, more than half of the students in the sample did record at least one journal entry most weeks. Just under one-third of students failed to write in their journals consistently, missing several weeks.

After examining students' individual entries, it became apparent that some students described more than one experience at a time. For instance, it was not uncommon for students to record a couple of different experiences that occurred during the day which they recorded in the one journal entry. To proceed with data analysis, individual students' journal entries were divided into experiences and each experience was numbered. For example, 24 experiences were identified for student A over the ten-week period, while for student K, only 7 experiences were identified. Across the 16 students' diary entries, a total of 207 student experiences were identified and then analysed following Giorgi's data analysis process so that 207 situated structural statements were compiled for each of the 207 student experiences.

From these 207 specific or structural statements, tentative themes emerged. Seven essential themes which generated the general descriptions or statements were confirmed by cross checking them against the tentative themes. The next part of the discussion discusses the seven essential themes and their general statements or descriptions.

Findings

The seven essential themes that emerged from the study were:

1. Schools support transition through programs and activities
2. Peers are significant others who can help or hinder a smooth transition from primary to high school
3. New procedures, locations and routines need to be learned in a new environment
4. Learning occurs through academic, practical and extracurricular activities and some learning is more challenging than other types of learning
5. Feelings of confidence, success and achievement can enhance high school transition
6. Homework/assignments are a challenging and necessary component of the high school curriculum
7. Teachers' attitudes/abilities can affect student integration into high school and make learning fun or boring

Schools Support Transition through Programs and Activities

Schools support transition through a number of programs and activities to help students adapt to the new environment. One such program is Peer Support where each Year 11 Peer Support leader acts as a buddy to a group of ten Year 7 students, paving the way to a smooth transition. The program enables students to meet and get to know other Year 7 students, fostering and developing new relationships amongst them. The friendly and informative support of the Peer Support leaders eases transition and allows Year 7 students to feel safe. The Year 7 Camp enables new friendships to be fostered and provides opportunities to strengthen friendships with existing friends. A private area within the school grounds is set aside for the exclusive use of Year 7 students outside class time. Teachers explain the workings of the timetable and engage students in games, group work and extracurricular activities that help them make new friends, thus reducing the stress of the new environment.

Peers are Significant Others Who Can Help or Hinder a Smooth Transition from Primary to High School

Peers play a significant role in enabling a smooth transition to high school. Friendship is important for survival in high school. Knowing others from primary school helps students feel safe and less nervous particularly in the early days and weeks of high school. When students see familiar faces amongst so many unfamiliar faces, they feel more confident and able to cope in the new environment. Friends help each other in difficult situations by being aware of their needs and also by providing support when certain academic work is too challenging. Friends help each other survive uninteresting lessons. To feel confident in the new environment, students like at least one friend to be with whether it is during class time, breaks or to participate in lunch time activities.

It is easy to make new friends in high school because the student population is very large when compared to the smallness of primary schools. The Peer Support program enables students to get to know many other students. Being the youngest members of the school means some students feel the need for the support of their friends to cope in an environment where others are older. Problems can occur when students face older peers who are rude and unhelpful. For some students, not being bullied by other and older students came as a pleasant surprise. Although an infrequent occurrence, bullying when experienced is both unsettling and upsetting for students.

Friendship groups can change on entering high school as not all students stay in the same primary school friendship groups and new friendships evolve and develop. This results in others having to establish new friends as well. High school is not only about making new friends; unfortunately it is also about losing some old friends.

New Procedures, Locations and Routines Need to Be Learned in a New Environment

Students are required to learn new procedures, location of rooms and other new routines in this environment. High school students follow a set timetable each day. Students are required to learn to read this timetable. The timetable is not user-friendly and a great challenge because it is in a coded form. By not being able to read and understand the timetable accurately some students bring the wrong books to class, get mixed up with their subjects, look disorganised and feel inadequate. The diary provided by the school is designed to assist in the interpretation of the timetable, but in the early weeks of the term failed to achieve this.

There are many subjects in high school and as a result many books to carry each day. There is also the added pressure of carrying the right books each day. Lockers provide a handy solution to carrying heavy bags all day long. However, the lockers are not situated anywhere close to the Year 7 Area. High school is a noisy place because there are so many teachers and students in the population unlike primary schools that are much smaller in nature.

Students need to be familiar with the new school rules very quickly to avoid getting into trouble with their teachers and disappointing them. Some face anxiety because high school is a highly organised institution and they need to learn organisational skills to survive and be part of the new environment. Catching public transport and getting used to train and bus timetables are a new experience for many and given time they expect to be familiar with it. Being in a single-sex school is another new experience for some students.

Learning Occurs Through the Academic, Practical and Extracurricular Activities and Some Learning is More Challenging Than Other Types of Learning

Learning occurs in a number of ways in high school. There are many academic subjects taught and many classes to attend. Some students find this exhausting while others are thrilled by this new experience. Some subjects are harder to understand than others mainly because they are unfamiliar. Students who learn these subjects in an interactive and interesting manner find it easier to cope with them. Learning new subjects with teachers who provide extra academic and moral support makes it easier to meet the challenge.

Invited speakers from outside the school enhance the learning program in the school. This adds variety to the school day making it interesting and informative. Practical lessons and extra-curricular activities enhance the learning process by teaching self-confidence, leadership skills, group work ethics, teamwork, character building and co-operation. These activities make learning more meaningful because they teach students to get to know others and assist them to build new friendships and positive relationships with their peers.

Students find easy subjects 'good' and difficult subjects 'bad'. The easy subjects are the ones that are interesting and activity based and not teacher or purely content centred. The academic subjects in high school teach students many new skills not previously taught in the primary school curriculum. Continual assessments are a part of high school curriculum. Students realise to be successful they need to practise, meet learning deadlines and revise regularly. High school curriculum is varied and can be challenging for many. The learning style expected of students in high school differs from primary school.

Feelings of Confidence, Success and Achievement Can Enhance High School Transition

High school transition is enhanced when students are confident and feel a sense of achievement and success in their new environment. Students are confident of surviving in the new environment when the support of at least one friend is available. Knowing peers from primary school makes students feel that they are not alone. Recognition of work by other peers boosts their self confidence and ability to adapt to the school. Students feel they have a sense of belonging when they are able to move around the school independently. Good and helpful teachers and friends build positive feelings and boost their confidence. Knowing others' names makes them confident of making friends easily.

Lack of confidence in the new school environment can result in making the transition harder for many. They do not know where to go and what to do especially on the first day which upsets some. Students realise that once they are over the confusion of the new environment high school will get easier to manage. Students find homework new to them and this has affected their confidence in succeeding easily. Not being organised affects their ability to complete work therefore achieving their goals. Lack of respect from other students for being the youngest and not holding a position of authority affects students' confidence.

Students need rewards to verify their success and achievements, giving them the ability to believe in themselves. Being praised for good work and high standards by teachers makes students feel positive about themselves and when they are able to complete their tasks it helps them feel successful. A lack of achievement occurs when students are not able to submit work and meet learning deadlines. This then affects students' ability to feel confident about their potential success in the new environment. Success is important to high school survival and integration.

Homework/Assignments are a Challenging and Necessary Component of the High School Curriculum

Homework and assignments are a part of the high school curriculum. Students find the volume of homework is far greater than what they received at primary school. The students do not find the homework difficult; it is the amount of homework given which poses a serious concern. The teachers give their own work without checking with the other teachers what the workload for students is and this lack of coordination among the staff/faculties frustrates students.

Besides the daily homework given, students also receive assignments/projects to complete. Students find these assignments far too challenging because many of them are given at the same time and they overlap with other subjects in terms of the deadlines unlike primary school where only one is given at a time. High school is a fun experience except for the amount of homework and constant assignments.

Teachers' Attitudes/Abilities Can Affect Student Integration into High School and Make Learning Fun or Boring

Teachers play a crucial role in making transition easier for students by assisting them with the integration into high school. They provide opportunities for students to get to know others in their class through games that teach about friendship. They build students' confidence by making them realise that changes during puberty are faced by all and they are never alone. Students prefer female teachers to teach subjects relating to puberty because they find female teachers more approachable and are less embarrassed. Students find pleasant, helpful and kind teachers more approachable. These teachers enhance learning by making learning easier, interesting and less stressful. Lessons that are interactive and practical are more meaningful and enjoyable for students. Students prefer to have many teachers because there will be some nicer ones amongst them they can approach for assistance. Teachers support students by allaying their fears regarding high school procedures and through their encouragement, students find it easier to achieve their potential as well as overcome academic difficulties.

When teachers are too strict and unfriendly, students find it harder to approach them. Teachers who are intolerant of late comers to class because they have lost their way put unnecessary pressure on them. Teachers who get annoyed with students who bring the wrong books to class because students cannot read the timetable accurately cause them to become upset and frustrated.

Students want to succeed academically in high school and find that teachers who do not explain concepts clearly and who are unapproachable inhibit learning while kind and competent teachers make it easier. Teachers with low expectations of their students' academic ability hinder students' learning and achievement. Students are confused by the different standards of discipline, rules and expectations of teachers from class to class and this lack of uniformity among teachers makes it harder for them to understand the expectations of the new environment.

Discussion

The findings of the current study revealed that students face many challenges during transition into high school and, at the same time, experience many positive aspects of transition. This study revealed a consistency with other projects that have examined students' transition into high school. As with many prior studies, the students in this sample found that it was a challenge to locate places/rooms in a new environment and they had difficulty reading the timetable. They found it stressful when they were lost in the school and became late for classes. They also worried about friendship. The positive experiences saw them enjoying being with friends and learning new and interesting things. Although the findings in the current study mirrored much of the previous literature on transition into high school, four key findings have been selected for further discussion because of the significant messages they provide to educators who are responsible for working with new high school students. These findings include the role of friendship, bullying, teachers' roles and homework.

Friendship

This study found that students on entering high school could end up losing their friends from primary school and this was unanticipated by students. Students learned that friends can be fickle and some were disappointed when previous long-standing friendships formed during their primary school years ended so abruptly. Many of the students in the study reported that their best friends were no longer their friends. These valued friends of many years chose to seek new friendships. In support of this finding, Cauley and Jovanovich (2006) argued that middle school transition can disrupt friendships in a number of ways. Firstly, when students attend a different high school from their friends; secondly when they attend the same high school but are placed in a different class; and thirdly when either party chooses not to have too much contact with the other.

In the current study, while students were disappointed by the loss of their best friends they also managed to make new friends without too much difficulty. They found it easy because high school was a bigger place with a greater enrolment of students as compared to their primary school. Unlike other studies (Hatton, 1995; Johnstone, 2001) where students had difficulty penetrating large, complex organisational structures making transition more difficult, here the size of the high school worked to the students' advantage. While other studies (e.g. see Green, 1997; Elias, 2002; Hinebauch, 2002) found students had difficulties making friends in their new environment, the students in the current study found the big school was an advantage because there were more people to make friends.

The students in this study were unprepared for the change in friendship groups and the development of new friendships, indicating that teachers in high schools should be aware of the fragility of friendship. Teachers have a responsibility to assist Year 7 students by providing them with opportunities to meet, develop and promote new friendships in their classes through learning and extracurricular activities. By using a variety of strategies to encourage students to get to know each other particularly in the early part of the year, teachers in this study did assist students in the transition process.

In summary, the study has clearly shown that schooling is not just about learning the curriculum; the social aspect of schooling plays a critical role at this stage of students' lives. It is important that educationalists do not underestimate the centrality of students' peer relationships and the particular challenges faced by students who do not form friendships in school (Cauley & Jovanovich, 2006). The study has clarified that during transition into high school, friendship is key to making a successful school and academic life for many students.

Bullying

Although bullying has been identified as a big problem in many schools, this did not appear to be the case in this study. Only three of the 207 experiences emanating from the journal entries of 16 students in the study pointed to some form of bullying. This figure would suggest that bullying was not a common occurrence for these 16 students during transition into high school. As with Green's (1997) findings, the anticipation of being bullied was greater than the actual event. The current study revealed that most students expected to be bullied when they entered high school. They also expected to be harassed because they were now the youngest in the school and therefore the smallest in size and the lowest in the social order. Such feelings of insignificance possibly exacerbated their fears of being bullied.

Unlike past studies (Weldy, 1990; Arowosafe & Irvin, 1992; Hatton, 1995; Cumming & Cormack, 1996; Akos, 2002; Johnstone, 2002) which reported evidence of many students' experiences of bullying and intimidation at the hands of older students, there were no reported incidents of senior students bullying these Year 7s, only two older peers. That bullying did not emerge as an issue for the majority of students in the study may be explained, at least in part, by the school's peer support program whereby senior students played an important role in helping to socialise students. Thus, an important implication in this study was the implementation of peer support program which eased students' transition into their new environment and, at the same time, lessened the possibility of seniors being potential bullies. Whole school programs such as peer support programs and mentoring programs (Knipe & Hussey, 2004; Cauley & Jovanovich, 2006) have been identified in the middle years of schooling literature as important strategies in helping students make a smooth transition from primary to secondary school.

Pivotal Role of Teachers

Within the middle schooling literature (Keddie & Churchill, 2005; Wells, 2005; Carrington, 2006; Cauley & Jovanovich, 2006) and literature focusing specifically on transition into secondary school (Cumming & Cormack, 1996; Johnstone, 2001, 2002), the role of the teacher in supporting students and enhancing their learning has been underscored. In the current study, students found that teachers were very helpful as they assisted them in many ways. For example, they helped them to get to know other students in their classes, explained new procedures and routines and were there to support them when they needed academic guidance. Students in this study did not have the experience of being treated as 'babies' by their teachers. This was in contrast to other research (see Hatton, 1995; Green, 1997; Barratt, 1998; Yates, 1999) that revealed that students felt they were treated as 'insignificant', 'immature', or 'babies' by their teachers. It is important for all teachers therefore to recognise students' need to be treated as adolescents and not as immature individuals.

Students indicated that they enjoyed having many teachers because it meant they were exposed to a variety of personalities and approaches. Furthermore, they had a larger pool from which to draw if they needed help and support. These findings are in contrast to other studies (see Weldy, 1990; Cumming & Cormack, 1996; Green, 1997; Yates, 1999; Johnstone, 2002) which found that students did not enjoy the experience of having so many teachers and found it to be a problem. Middle schooling policy (Chadbourne, 2001; Luke *et al.*, 2003) also encourages the reduction in the number of teachers in the middle years; yet, this study indicates that students enjoyed having many teachers so that they could have access to at least one kind and supportive teacher and they would not be placed with an unkind/unhelpful teacher all the time. Reduction in number of teachers during transition may therefore not necessarily be the answer for an easier transition into high school. It is the consideration and caring nature of teachers that is of paramount importance for surviving high school transition for these adolescents according to this study.

As evident from previous research, this study supported other studies that have identified the key role of teachers, their need to be sensitive to the needs of newcomers and to realise that, for students, entering a new environment can be fraught with many challenges. Teachers need to remember to support students by giving them the time needed for high school adjustment and not rushing them. They must be aware that many of these students, initially at least, lack confidence, therefore tactfulness is required (van Manen, 1991). As Cumming and Cormack (1996) state, teachers who are not tactful could very well hinder high school integration and cause alienation and disengagement. Teachers could benefit by training in the area of adolescent development to better support this age group (Cumming & Cormack, 1996; Barratt, 1998).

Homework and Assignments

Past research conducted in Australia (Kirkpatrick, 1992; Hatton, 1995; Yates, 1999) has found homework to be a major issue of concern among students entering high school, yet it seems that schools continue to have high expectations regarding the quality and quantity of homework completed by students. In this study, students were concerned that they were overloaded with homework/assignments. Interestingly, it was not the level of difficulty of the homework but the sheer volume of it coupled with unrealistic deadlines. Students blamed this overload on poor coordination among their teachers. Attempting both homework and assignments was a great struggle which was beyond the capacity of many.

It is evident that there is a need for coordination among teachers when planning and setting assignments and other tasks required by students outside of class hours. Such coordination could help to ensure that students are not overloaded with too many tasks at the one time. Teachers need to meet and discuss when each faculty is setting homework and assignments and the due dates for each. This rather simple process would ensure that the workload is spread out for the students and would avoid overlapping. For secondary schools that uphold middle schooling practices of collaborative team teaching and planning and integrated curriculum and pedagogy (Westcombe-Down, 2004; Wells, 2005; Carrington, 2006) it is anticipated that teachers would automatically coordinate homework and assignment due dates because they would be planning and working together, at least for some of the time. Yet it was evident from students' journal entries that they had been exposed to more traditional sets of school practices (i.e. discipline based subjects taught by individual specialist teachers in specific rooms) rather than those advocated by middle schooling experts. This was unsurprising given that students were enrolled in a New South Wales government school. As discussed previously, the dominant approach to middle years reform taken by the Education Department in New South Wales has been one focusing on 'transition' (Luke *et al.*, 2003) rather than those broader philosophical educational issues posed by contemporary middle schooling literature.

In the context of the present study, emphasis should be placed on the quality of homework and not the quantity of homework. An important implication for the school in which the study took place is the need for teachers and administrators to re-examine the School's Homework Policy to see if it best reflects the interests and needs of students. Second, it might be appropriate to incorporate a component on developing organisational skills within the existing program to help students meet their learning deadlines. Homework, then, is an important area to consider during transition as it emerged in this study and other studies (Hatton, 1995; Yates, 1999; Johnstone, 2002) as a key issue of concern for students.

Conclusion

In this study, students' experiences of transition into secondary school were investigated utilising a phenomenological psychological research approach. This methodology showed itself to be appropriate for studying students' transition into high school as an important human experience. A significant contribution of this study was that it used a methodology which tends not to be used widely in educational research yet has great potential for gaining a deeper understanding of human experience. In contrast to other qualitative research approaches, phenomenology requires the researcher to view things not only from the point of view of the subject, but to study in subjects, the object of their experience (Crotty, 1996). In other words, phenomenology elucidates not only *how* people experience but '*what* people experience' (Crotty, 1996, p. 3, original italics). In this study, a phenomenological psychological approach enabled a movement from understanding 16 students' experiences of being in high school for the first 10 weeks to insights which revealed what makes being in high school during the initial transitionary period what it is. Finally, another important contribution of phenomenological research is its moral dimension. As van Manen (1997) reminds us, 'phenomenological research carries a moral force' (p. 12) which means that it is the moral responsibility of educators to find out more about students' experiences of phenomena in order to facilitate and better support their learning and development.

The results of this study suggest that the tensions caused by transition into high school can be lessened if there is sufficient support given to students by their peers, high school teachers and older peers. Support via the introduction of programs and targeted activities designed to enhance students' sense of belonging and reduce their fear of the new environment can also go a long way to minimising transitional difficulties. Furthermore, this study has shown that much rests in the hands of a school's community—peers, teachers and administrators—to make transition into high school a relatively smooth and stress-free experience for new high school students.

References

Akos, P. (2002) Student Perceptions of the Transition from Elementary to Middle School, *Professional School Counseling*, 5:5, pp. 339–346.

Arowosafe, D. & Irvin, J. L. (1992) Transition to a Middle Level School: What kids say, *Middle School Journal*, 24:2, pp. 15–19.

Barratt, R. (1998) *Shaping Middle Schooling in Australia: A report of the national middle schooling project* (Canberra, Australian Curriculum Studies Association).

Beane, J. (1991) The Middle School: The natural home of integrated curriculum, *Educational Leadership*, 49:2, pp. 9–13.

Carrington, V. (2006) *Rethinking Middle Years: Early adolescents, schooling and digital culture* (Crows Nest, NSW, Allen & Unwin).

Cauley, K. M. & Jovanovich, D. (2006) Developing an Effective Transition Program for Students Entering Middle School or High School, *Clearing House*, 80:1, pp. 15–25.

Chadbourne, R. (2001) *Middle Schooling for the Middle Years: What might the jury be considering?* (Melbourne, Australian Education Union).

Cormack, P. (1991) *The Nature of Adolescence* (Adelaide, Education Department of South Australia).

Cotterell, J. L. (1982) Student Experiences Following Entry into Secondary School, *Educational Research*, 24:4, pp. 296–302.

Cotterell, J. L. (2002) Standard Gauge, *Australian Journal of Middle Schooling*, 2:1, pp. 7–12.

Crotty, M. (1996) *Phenomenology and Nursing Research* (South Melbourne, Churchill Livingstone).

Cumming, J. & Cormack, P. (1996) *From Alienation to Engagement: Opportunities for reform in the middle years of schooling (vols. 1,2,3)* (Canberra, Australian Curriculum Studies Association).

Cumming, J. (ed.) (1996) *Opportunities for Reform in the Middle School* (vol. 3) (Canberra, Australian Curriculum Studies Association).

Department of Education and Training, NSW (2003) *Statistical Bulletin, Schools and Students in New South Wales 2002*. Retrieved February 14, 2003, from www.det.nsw.edu.au

Dockett, S. & Perry, B. (1999a) Starting School: What do children say? *Early Child Development & Care*, 159, pp. 107–119.

Dockett, S. & Perry, B. (1999b) Starting School: What matters for children, parents and educators? *AECA Research in Practice Series*, 6:3, pp. 1–18.

Dockett, S. & Perry, B. (2001) *Starting School: Effective transitions*, Retrieved November 17, 2003, from www.ecrp.uiuc.edu/v3n2/dockett.html

Dockett, S. & Perry, B. (2003) The Transition to School: What's important, *Educational Leadership*, 60:7, pp. 30–33.

Dockett, S., Perry, B., Howard, P., Whitton, D. & Cusack, M. (2002) Australian Children Starting School, *Childhood Education*, 78:6, pp. 349–353.

Early, D. M., Pianta, R. C. & Cox, M. J. (1999) Kindergarten Teachers and Classrooms: A transition context, *Early Education and Development*, 10:1, pp. 25–46.

Education Queensland. (2001) *Middle Phase of Learning*. Retrieved November 17, *2004*, from www.education.qld.gov.au

Ehrich, L. C. (1998) Principals' Experiences of the Professional Development of Teachers, in: L. C. Ehrich & J. Knight (eds), *Leadership in Crisis? Restructuring principled practice* (Flaxton, QLD, Post Pressed).

Elias, M. J. (2002) Transitioning to Middle School, *The Education Digest*, 67:8, pp. 41–43.

Gattis, J. (1995) *Erikson's Psychosocial Stages of Development*. Retrieved August 2, 2003, from www.students.biola.edu

Giorgi, A. P. (1985a) The Phenomenological Psychology of Learning and the Verbal Learning Tradition, in: A. P. Giorgi (ed.), *Phenomenology and Psychological Research* (Pittsburg, PA, Duquesne University Press).

Giorgi, A. P. (1985b) Sketch of a Psychological Phenomenological Method, in: A. P. Giorgi (ed.), *Phenomenology and Psychological Research* (Pittsburgh, PA, Duquesne University Press).

Giorgi, A., Fischer, W. F. & von Eckartsberg, R. (eds) (1971) *Duquesne Studies in Phenomenological Psychology (vol. 1)* (Pittsburgh, PA, Duquesne University Press and Humanities Press).

Green, P. (1997) Moving from the World of the Known to the Unknown: The transition from primary to secondary school, *Melbourne Studies in Education*, 38:2, pp. 67–84.

Hatton, E. (1995) Middle School Students' Perceptions of School Organisation, *Unicorn*, 21:3, pp. 17–26.

Hertzog, C. J. & Morgan, P. L. (1998) Breaking the Barriers between Middle School and High School: Developing a transition team for student success, *National Association of Secondary School Principals Bulletin*, 82:597, pp. 94–98.

Hinebauch, S. (2002) Nurturing the Emerging Independent Adolescent, *Independent School*, 61:4, pp. 12–17.

Husserl, E. (1970) *Logical Investigations*, J. N. Findlay, trans., Vol. 1 (New York, Humanities Press) (Original work published 1900).

Husserl, E. (1971) *Phenomenology*, R. E. Palmer, trans. Retrieved August 2, 2003, from www.stanford.edu (Original work published 1927 in Encyclopaedia Britannica).

Johnstone, K. (2001) *The Lived Reality of the Transition to High School for Rural Students*. Paper presented at the Australian Association of Research in Education (Fremantle, WA).

Johnstone, K. (2002) *The Transition into High School: A journey of uncertainty*. Paper presented at the Australian Association of Research in Education (Brisbane, QLD).

Kaplan, L. S. (1996) Where's your Focus? High academic standards versus personal social development, *National Association of Secondary School Principals Bulletin*, 6:1, pp. 6–10.

Keddie, A. & Churchill, R. (2005) Teacher-Student Relationships, in: D. Pendergast & N. Bahr (eds), *Teaching Middle Years: Rethinking curriculum, pedagogy and assessment* (Crows Nest, NSW, Allen & Unwin).

Kiloh, B. & Morris, G. (2000) A Systems Approach to Dealing with Middle School Issues, *Ethos*, 8:1, pp. 7–12.

Kirkpatrick, D. (1992) *Student Perceptions of the Transition from Primary to Secondary School*. Paper presented at the Australian Association of Research in Education/New Zealand Association of Research in Education (Geelong, VIC).

Knipe, S. & Hussey, R. (2004) Building a Relationship through Transition, *Primary & Middle Years Educator*, 2:2, pp. 11–13.

La Rue, A., Raymond, A. & Weiss, R. G. (2004) *Essentials for Success in Preschool and Beyond*. Retrieved November 10, 2003, from www.apa.org

Legters, N. & Kerr, K. (2001) *The Effects of Transition to High School: An investigation of reform practices to promote ninth grade success* (Cambridge, MA, John Hopkins University).

Luke, A., Elkins, J., Weir, K., Land, R., Carrington, V., Dole, S., Pendergast, D., Kapitzke, C., van Kraayenoord, C., Moni, K., McIntosh, A., Mayer, D., Bahr, N., Hunter, L., Chadbourne, R., Bean, T., Alverman, D. & Stevens, L. (2003) *Beyond the Middle: A report about literacy and numeracy development of target group students in the middle years of schooling* (vol. 1) (Brisbane, J.S. McMillan Printing Group).

Manning, M. L. (2000) Child-Centered Middle Schools, *Childhood Education*, 76:3, pp. 154–159.

Meece, J. L. (2002) *Child and Adolescent Development for Educators* (2nd edn.) (New York, McGraw Hill).

Merleau-Ponty, M. (1962) *The Phenomenology of Perception* (C. Smith, trans.) (New York, Humanities Press).

Mizelle, N. B. (1999) Helping Middle School Students Making the Transition into High School, *ERIC Clearing House on Elementary and Early Childhood Education Champaign IL*.

Mizelle, N. B. & Irvin, J. L. (2000) *Transition from Middle School into High School*. Retrieved March 15, 2003, from www.nmsa.org

Mullins, E. R. & Irvin, J. L. (2000) Transition into Middle School, *Middle School Journal*, 31:3, pp. 58–60.

Patton, M. Q. (1990) *Qualitative Evaluation and Research Methods* (2nd edn.) (Newbury Park, CA, Sage).

Pendergast, D. (2005) The Emergence of Middle Schooling, in: D. Pendergast & N. Bahr (eds), *Teaching Middle Years: Rethinking curriculum, pedagogy and assessment* (Crows Nest, NSW, Allen & Unwin).

Polkinghorne, D. E. (1989) Phenomenological Research Methods, in: R. S. Valle & S. Halling (eds), *Existential Phenomenological Perspectives in Psychology* (New York, Plenum Press).

Simmons, R. G. & Blyth, D. A. (1987) *Moving into Adolescence: The impact of pubertal change and school context* (New York, Aldine de Gruyter).

Spinelli, E. (1989) *The Interpreted World: An introduction to phenomenological psychology* (London, Sage).

Tesch, R. (1984) *Phenomenological Studies: A critical analysis of their nature and procedures*. Paper presented at the American Educational Research Association Annual Meeting (New Orleans, LA).

Tonkin, S. E. & Watt, H. M. G. (2003) Self-concept over the Transition from Primary to

Secondary School: A case study on a program for girls, *Issues in Educational Research*, 13:2, pp. 27–54.

Urdan, T., Midgley, C. & Wood, S. (1995) Special Issues in Reforming Middle Level Schools, *Journal of Early Adolescence*, 15:1, pp. 9–37.

van Manen, M. (1991) *The Tact of Teaching: The meaning of pedagogical thoughtfulness* (Albany, State University of New York Press).

van Manen, M. (1997) *Researching Lived Experience: Human science for an action sensitive pedagogy* (2nd edn.) (Ontario, The Althouse Press).

Walker, M. (2002) From Junior High to Middle School: Orchestrating the Punahou transition, *Independent School*, 61:4, pp. 10–15.

Weldy, G. R. (1990) Stronger School Transitions Improve Student Achievement: A Bulletin special, *National Association of Secondary School Principals Bulletin*, 74:523, pp. 60–73.

Wells, C. (2005) Structuring Assessment in the Middle Years: So this is who I am?, *Primary & Middle Years Educator*, 3:1, pp. 22–27.

Westcombe-Down, D. (2004) Educational Ergonomics for Middle Schooling in Catholic Education: Work in progress, *South Australian Science Teachers Association (SASTA) Journal*, 1, pp. 30–31.

Yates, L. (1999) Transitions and the Year 7 Experience: A report from the 12 to 18 project, *Australian Journal of Education*, 43:1, pp. 24–41.

Index